“Many readers, since the Old Testament is so long, lose track of the story after Deuteronomy. Ian J. Vaillancourt expertly guides us on a tour from Joshua through Ezra–Nehemiah, unfolding for us the story of God’s redeeming purposes. Vaillancourt reads Old Testament texts in their historical context and canonically in light of their fulfillment in Christ. A most helpful and compact survey!”

Thomas Schreiner, James Buchanan Harrison Professor of New Testament Interpretation at The Southern Baptist Theological Seminary

“In this wonderful primer, Ian J. Vaillancourt skillfully uncovers the many riches of the Old Testament story and shows us the many ways this story—in its twists and turns—points us to Christ. Vaillancourt brings together the expertise of an Old Testament scholar, the gifts of an experienced teacher, and the heart of a pastor to give us a theologically rich and spiritually enriching introduction to the Old Testament’s Historical Books. This book is a real treasure. I highly recommend it!”

Uche Anizor, professor of theology at the Talbot School of Theology at Biola University

“For too many of us, the Old Testament has no more shape than a dismembered skeleton, a pile of bones on the floor. We need someone to put it back together and show us its shape and function. We may have heard brilliant sermons on a single Bible verse or chapter, even a helpful series of sermons on one Bible book, but until now, we have not received help that we need to grasp the meaning of the Bible as a whole. In this brilliantly clear and insightful book, *Unfolding Redemption*, Ian J. Vaillancourt comes to our rescue. He takes us through the Historical Books and the prophetic books and enables us to see the Old Testament as one story of redemption that reaches its intended goal in the redeeming work of Jesus Christ. We are in his debt.”

Gregory Goswell, adjunct lecturer in Old Testament at Christ College

“I highly recommend this engaging overview of the Former Prophets and Latter Writings. Ian J. Vaillancourt blends crisp prose, rich exegesis, and compelling theological synthesis to equip readers to grasp the glorious message of these challenging Old Testament books.”

Brian J. Tabb, president and professor of biblical studies at Bethlehem College and Seminary

“Ian J. Vaillancourt follows up his work on the Pentateuch, *The Dawning of Redemption*, with an excellent treatment of the rest of the Old Testament. While the collection of books in the Old Testament may seem diverse and random, Vaillancourt shows that there is a single plot structure and storyline from a single divine mind unfolding God’s plan of redemption. Designed as an entry-level exposition, this book is highly recommended to help get into the Old Testament and the story of Scripture itself.”

Peter J. Gentry, senior professor at The Southern Baptist Theological Seminary

"Building off the dawn of redemptive hope in Moses' five books, the rest of the Old Testament highlights the development of this future-oriented faith by detailing how God settled, delivered, led, represented, warned, and punished his redeemed. Yet it also clarifies how God extended, preserved, partially restored, and promised to deliver them fully through the long-awaited redeemer. Ian J. Vaillancourt's *Unfolding Redemption* compellingly overviews this progressing drama of salvation and faithfully shows how it all climaxes in Jesus Christ."

Jason S. DeRouchie, research professor of Old Testament and biblical theology and Rich and Judy Hastings Endowed Chair of Old Testament Studies at Midwestern Baptist Theological Seminary

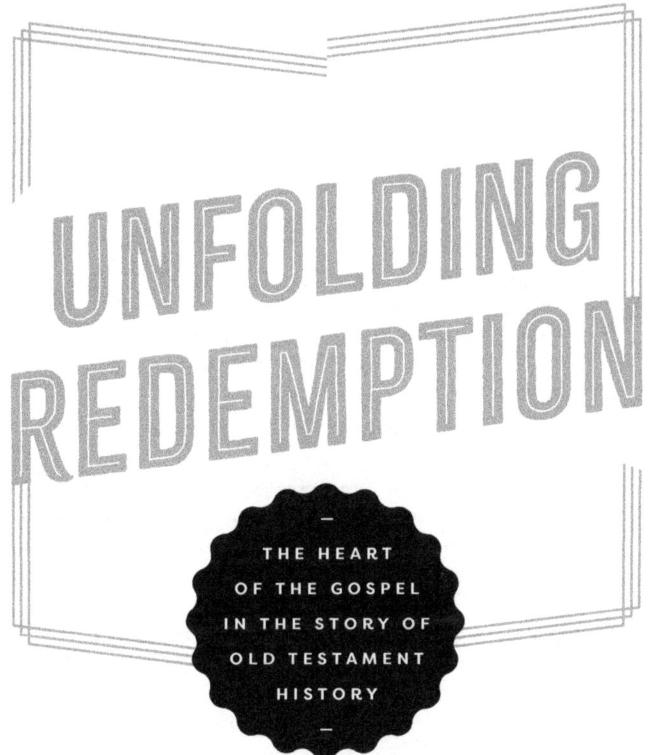

IAN J. VAILLANCOURT

An imprint of InterVarsity Press
Downers Grove, Illinois

InterVarsity Press
P.O. Box 1400 | Downers Grove, IL 60515-1426
ivpress.com | email@ivpress.com

InterVarsity Press® is the publishing division of InterVarsity Christian Fellowship/USA®. For more information, visit intervarsity.org.

Cover design: Faceout Studio, Tim Green
Interior design: Daniel van Loon

ISBN 978-1-5140-1154-6 (print) | ISBN 978-1-5140-1155-3 (digital)

Printed in the United States of America ♾

Library of Congress Cataloging-in-Publication Data
Names: Vaillancourt, Ian J. author
Title: Unfolding redemption : the heart of the Gospel in the story of Old Testament history / Ian J. Vaillancourt.
Description: Downers Grove, IL : IVP Academic, [2026] | Includes bibliographical references and index.
Identifiers: LCCN 2025038310 (print) | LCCN 2025038311 (ebook) | ISBN 9781514011546 paperback | ISBN 9781514011553 ebook
Subjects: LCSH: Bible. Historical Books–Criticism, interpretation, etc. | Bible. Historical Books–Relation to Gospels | Bible. Gospels–Relation to Historical books | Redemption–Biblical teaching
Classification: LCC BS1205.52 .V35 2026 (print) | LCC BS1205.52 (ebook)
LC record available at https://lccn.loc.gov/2025038310
LC ebook record available at https://lccn.loc.gov/2025038311

32 31 30 29 28 27 26 | 13 12 11 10 9 8 7 6 5 4 3 2 1

To my mom and stepdad,

Joyce and Don McPherson;

my dad and stepmom,

Bruce and Cathy Vaillancourt;

and my father-in-law and mother-in-law,

Ekkehard and Nancy Heidebrecht.

And in loving memory of my grandparents,

Elgin and Emily Stott

and

Bruce and Olive Vaillancourt;

and my grandparents-in-law,

Cornelius and Greta Heidebrecht

and

Bill and Cora Nicholls.

You have all sacrificed to bless our family in countless ways.

We thank God for all of you!

CONTENTS

PREFACE

THIS IS A BOOK ABOUT the Old Testament story that flows out of the Pentateuch and leads into the New Testament. I have written another book called *The Dawning of Redemption: The Story of the Pentateuch and the Hope of the Gospel* (Crossway, 2022). It is meant to equip readers to dig deeply into the first five books of the Old Testament on their own. This book is not a sequel, in the sense that you do not need to have read *Dawning* in order to benefit from this book. Whether readers are thoughtful Christians, students, or pastors, this book will accomplish its goal if it equips Christians to study God's Word in a deeper way. But if you find this book helpful, you are invited to read *Dawning* as well: Together, *Dawning* and *Unfolding* provide a big-picture primer on the entire Old Testament story.

Before we dive in, asking and answering three questions will help readers get on the same page:[1]

1. What does *YHWH* mean, and why does this vowel-free word appear so often in this book?
2. What does *torah* mean, and why does this word appear in this book?
3. Which Bible version does this book primarily employ?

[1]From this point forward, this preface is adapted from (or is quoting directly from) the preface of Ian J. Vaillancourt, *The Dawning of Redemption: The Story of the Pentateuch and the Hope of the Gospel* (Crossway, 2022). Used by permission.

We'll briefly answer each of these questions in turn.

First, what does *YHWH* mean? The personal name for God in the Old Testament is often spelled YHWH and pronounced Yahweh. Although most English Bibles use the *title* "the LORD" for this Hebrew word, in this book we will use *YHWH*, except when I am quoting from an English Bible. This will give us practice: We can make the switch from *the LORD* to *YHWH* in our minds as we encounter Old Testament citations, and hopefully this new habit will spill over to our personal reading of the Old Testament. Since the name YHWH appears 6,828 times in the Old Testament, this practice will help to emphasize the personal nature of God, because he revealed himself by his personal name.

Second, what does *torah* mean? *Torah* is a Hebrew word that is usually (imperfectly) translated as "law" in English Bibles. Since this word does not have an exact English equivalent, we will use *torah* or *instruction* instead of *law*, except when I am quoting from an English Bible. So when you encounter "the law" in a direct citation of the Old Testament, I encourage you to supply *torah* or *instruction*. This will help us remember that this Hebrew word means much more than the rules that our English word *law* usually calls to mind: It has the more positive meaning of "instruction" for how to live as God's people. Additionally, when *Torah* is capitalized mid-sentence, it is being used as a title for the first five books of the Old Testament.

Third, unless otherwise indicated, all Scripture citations have been taken from the English Standard Version (ESV). Although there are many excellent English translations of the Bible, the preface to the ESV describes it as "essentially literal," and thus its nature is a bit more suited to a study like this one because it will help us notice details in God's Word.

INTRODUCTION

GETTING ORIENTED TO AN OUT-OF-ORDER REDEMPTION STORY

He was unable to walk, and he had lived with his disability for nearly four decades. Then a passerby changed his life in an instant. This man told him to take up his bed and walk, and he was instantly healed! But in the midst of this man's joy, he found himself, of all things, in a controversy about how to interpret the Old Testament.

The Jewish leaders immediately disregarded the miracle and scorned the man for taking up his bed on the Sabbath—they claimed these actions were out of step with the Old Testament. But Jesus (the healer) contested this. According to Jesus, the Jewish leaders were *misinterpreting* the Old Testament. In the interchange that followed, Jesus called God his own father, making himself equal with God. He also made reference to his role in a coming resurrection and judgment. Then he made another audacious claim: "You search the Scriptures because you think that in them you have eternal life; and it is they that bear witness about me, yet you refuse to come to me that you may have life" (Jn 5:39-40).

Do we hear what Jesus was saying? The Jewish leaders were experts in the Scriptures—what Christians today call the Old Testament. But Jesus was telling these highly educated teachers of the Bible that they didn't have a clue: They thought their interpretation of the Old Testament was enough to receive eternal life. But the Old Testament bears witness *about Jesus*, and these people refused to come *to Jesus* to have life. According to Jesus, it is possible to be a world-renowned Bible expert and miss out on eternal life. If we spend our lives studying the Old Testament story and we are not led to Jesus, the results will be devastating.

This is a book about the story of the Old Testament beyond its beginning. While the five books of the Pentateuch make up the essential first act in the Bible's grand story of redemption, a lot more story is told before we reach its climax in Jesus Christ. The story that flows out of the Pentateuch is the link from the Bible's first act to the New Testament. As we are gripped by the unfolding story of redemption that continues after the Pentateuch, and as we notice some of the many links between this story and its fulfillment in Christ, we will grasp the gospel more deeply and treasure Jesus more than ever.

Even in an initial reading, we discover many wonderful truths in Joshua, Judges, Samuel, Kings, Ruth, Daniel, Esther, Ezra–Nehemiah, and Chronicles.[1] In these books we witness YHWH dwelling among his people in the special land he had promised them many years before. We see leaders raised up to deliver God's people and incline their hearts back to him. We also encounter a great prophet named Samuel, a great king in David, and a great deliverance over Goliath—who doesn't love that amazing story? In these books, a temple is built to replace the tent-structure where YHWH had been dwelling—Israel's settledness in their own land meant they could have a more permanent place where YHWH's glory would settle among his people. And after the horrible tragedy of exile, we witness YHWH's

---

[1]Since 1–2 Samuel, 1–2 Kings, and 1–2 Chronicles were each separated into two parts because of the limits of scroll length, it is acceptable to use *Samuel, Kings*, and *Chronicles* as shorthand for these two-part works. Similarly, the books of Ezra and Nehemiah are hyphenated as Ezra–Nehemiah because they are read as one book in the Hebrew Old Testament. The order of books listed here will be explained as this introduction progresses.

faithfulness to his people as they live outside the Promised Land, along with his power in bringing them back. From beginning to end, the Old Testament story highlights the faithfulness and goodness of God.

If we're honest, though, many of us struggle to stay engaged as we encounter these books chapter by chapter. We might ask why the book of Joshua spends *nine chapters* recording minute geographical details about the land inheritance for each tribe of Israel. We might also ask why 1 Chronicles begins with *nine chapters* of genealogy. These long sections of God's Word have led many to (mistakenly) conclude that the Old Testament is impractical, the reading equivalent of spinach at suppertime—something we choke down because we have been told it is healthy, but the reading (or eating) experience is a sheer act of will.

More seriously, the holy wars in Joshua seem out of step with the New Testament command to love our neighbor. And a scene such as the grotesque sexual assault and dismembering of the Levite's concubine does not seem fit for polite company (Judg 19). In fact, the book of Judges draws a similar conclusion: "And all who saw it said, 'Such a thing has never happened or been seen from the day that the people of Israel came up out of the land of Egypt until this day; consider it, take counsel, and speak'" (Judg 19:30). If the scenes of holy war or the Levite's concubine were filmed as Netflix specials, viewer discretion would certainly be advised. So why are they in the Bible? Should we read these to our children? Is there anything in them to encourage us in our love for Christ, to urge us to share Christ, or to help us live for Christ?

The Jewish leaders who opposed Jesus were guilty of searching the (Old Testament) Scriptures but missing Jesus. Similarly, many Christians today experience the Old Testament as drudgery because the story *seems* so far removed from life in the twenty-first century, and the New Testament *feels* much more accessible and life giving.

Therefore, many are guilty of not reading the Old Testament and thus missing Jesus or of reading the Old Testament but not understanding it—so missing Jesus.

This book is like an aerial view on our smartphone's map app: It will help us gain a big-picture understanding of the Old Testament story and some of its links to Christ. This book is not meant to provide all the answers to every question we may have about the Old Testament story beyond the Pentateuch. It is, however, written to equip us to dive more deeply into these books on our own, experiencing life-transforming, gospel-saturated words of life. This is essential because, according to Jesus, the entire Old Testament testifies about him (see Lk 24:27, 44).

THE BIBLE'S GRAND STORY OF REDEMPTION

Before we dive into the middle part of the Bible's story of redemption, let's get a sense of the larger story.[2] The grand story of the Bible can be broken up into four uneven parts. In Genesis 1–2 we encounter the God of *creation*, with humanity as the crowning climax of his work—part one. Then, in Genesis 3, we learn about the *fall* into sin and all its effects—part two. The bulk of the Bible's story, from Genesis 3:15 to Revelation 20, tells the story of *redemption*, of the God who did not leave us in our sins but chose to rescue us from sin and all of its effects—part three. Finally, the last few chapters of the Bible revel in the *consummation*, when a return to a new and better Garden of Eden will finally be accomplished—part four. If we ever step into an elevator and are asked what the Bible is about, we now have a four-point, sixty-second sermon ready to go: creation, fall, redemption, consummation.

Since the story of redemption begins in Genesis 3:15 and finds its consummation at the end of Revelation, we can observe that most of

[2]For a more thorough summary of the story so far, see Ian J. Vaillancourt, *The Dawning of Redemption: The Story of the Pentateuch and the Hope of the Gospel* (Crossway, 2022).

the Bible's story is about *redemption*. And this grand story of redemption can be further broken up into three acts: the Pentateuch, the rest of the Old Testament story, and the climax in Christ.

Given that the Bible tells the grand story of *redemption*, it is important to be clear on what this word means. In the ancient world, *redemption* referred to the rescue of a person from a situation over which they were powerless, and the biblical authors fittingly use this word to describe the way God works for his people. For example, in the book of Exodus, God *redeems* Israel from their slavery in Egypt in order to make them his special people (see Ex 6:6-7; 19:5-6). The entire nation of God's people were helpless slaves, and YHWH came to redeem them *from* slavery and *to* himself—it was a physical and a spiritual rescue. Then, in the New Testament, the word *redemption* is used to describe God's work of delivering his people from spiritual bondage and to himself (e.g., Rom 3:24; Eph 1:7). This is accomplished by the death and resurrection of the Lord Jesus.[3]

THE DAWNING OF REDEMPTION

The Pentateuch begins the Bible's story of redemption by portraying creation as the theater of redemption (Gen 1), before the promise of redemption was first given in the Garden of Eden (Gen 3:15).[4] As the story continues, we encounter genealogies that trace the lineage of redemption, along with covenants between YHWH and his people—YHWH's guarantee of redemption (e.g., Gen 15). Next, the exodus from Egypt is the greatest act of redemption in the entire Old Testament. These people YHWH had rescued from Egypt are then given instructions about how to live as his redeemed people (Ex 19–24). They are also given directives about building a tabernacle where YHWH would dwell among them, priests would mediate between

[3]See Gary S. Shogren, "Redemption: New Testament," in *Anchor Bible Dictionary*, ed. David Noel Freedman (Doubleday, 1992), 5:654. Much of the content of this paragraph was gleaned from Vaillancourt, *Dawning of Redemption*, 30-31.

[4]This section briefly summarizes Vaillancourt, *Dawning of Redemption*.

YHWH and his people, and there would be a sacrificial system to make atonement for their sins. In the book of Numbers, the people fail to believe YHWH and so they wander in the wilderness for forty years. Finally, the book of Deuteronomy concludes with YHWH's redeemed people on the cusp of entering the Promised Land. Near the end of this book YHWH warns his people with a long list of blessings for covenant keeping, curses for covenant breaking, and restoration for covenant repentance (see Deut 28; 30:1-10; cf. Lev 26).

THE UNFOLDING OF REDEMPTION

These truths about blessings, curses, and restoration are especially helpful for understanding the Old Testament story that unfolds after the Pentateuch. When YHWH's redeemed people keep his covenant, they are lavished with blessings for covenant keeping (see Lev 26:3-13; Deut 28:1-14)—such as the Promised Land in the book of Joshua, David as king in the book of Samuel, and a temple in the book of Kings. On the other hand, when YHWH's redeemed people break the covenant, the curses for covenant breaking fall on them (see Lev 26:14-39; Deut 28:15-68)—especially in the destruction of the temple, the loss of a king in David's lineage, the people's exile from the Promised Land, and their sojourn in a land where no one worshiped YHWH.

As they bear these horrible curses, Deuteronomy 30:1-10 promises them restoration if they will only repent and turn back to YHWH (see also Lev 26:40-45). This explains why YHWH preserves his redeemed people as they sojourn in exile. It also explains why he opens the door for many of his people to return to their land, build a new temple, and begin to settle again. As we will see, this return had two sides: It was very much a blessing from the hand of their faithful God, but it also lacked the fullness that had been promised to them. The full and total restoration to an even better position than before would require a better temple, a greater king, and the ultimate dwelling place for God's people.

AN OUT-OF-ORDER REDEMPTION STORY

Out of order in two senses. The subtitle of this introduction is "Getting Oriented to an Out-of-Order Redemption Story." What does this mean? When a snack machine charges our credit card but our snack is not dispensed, the machine is out of order—it doesn't work as it should. The Old Testament redemption story is out of order in a related sense: It did not fully accomplish its desired outcome. The Old Testament story concludes with readers yearning for something better, something ultimate—something in step with the grandeur of its promises. The Old Testament doesn't tell the story of YHWH's redemption of a people and their subsequent onward and upward trajectory toward eternal riches in Christ. Instead, the Old Testament tells the story of a people who are pursued by a gracious God but choose to turn from him. So, the path to the Bible's ultimate climax is long and winding. This story is not out of order because of any fault in YHWH or his plan of redemption; it is out of order because of his people's hard hearts. This means that much of the story of the Old Testament will provide the dark velvet backdrop that will make the diamond of the gospel shine more brightly—when, in Christ, God will finally fix the world's brokenness and fulfill his promises.

But the story of the Old Testament is also out of order in another sense: It is like an excited child telling the story of their day at the fair. "You won't believe what happened," they exclaim as they hold up their giant stuffed animal. They begin by telling the story of winning their incredible toy, and then they share about their favorite snacks, rides, and games. Most adults hearing this will instinctively realize that they are not hearing a *this, then this, then this* chronological recounting of the day. Much the same, the Old Testament Historical Books are not always arranged in chronological order. As we will see, the Old

Testament story continues after the Pentateuch in a cluster of books, but then the story is paused as prophets, poets, and sages herald their message to God's people. The story picks up again with a cluster of books at the end of the Old Testament, and this leads us to anticipate Christ even more. Along the way, books are sometimes taken out of chronological order, so we hear the most important themes and emphases of the unfolding story more clearly.

Two kinds of Old Testament books beyond the Pentateuch. There are many Old Testament books that do not tell the *story* of God's people so much as speak a *message* to those same people. These include the written words of prophets, the poetic praise of psalmists, and the poetic tears of Lamentations. They also include the wisdom of sages, who taught God's people how to live skillfully in the real world with YHWH as their God.

But there are also many other Old Testament books that *selectively record real history with a focus on the continuing story of redemption.* These books record real history—they report what actually happened in the real history of the real world in which we live. But they also *selectively* record real history—the authors of these books did not record every event that ever happened in the history of the world. Instead, they were Holy Spirit–inspired storytellers who focused the message of their books on YHWH's unfolding story of redemption.

How does the Old Testament story unfold? Which Old Testament books cover this story, and how does it unfold? In table I.1 below, we compare the most common English order of Old Testament books with the earliest attested Hebrew order. In each column, I have marked the books that tell the continuing story of the Old Testament in italics. Although table I.1 reveals the same books for English and Hebrew, the order of books—and therefore the way the story unfolds—is quite different.

Table I.1. The unfolding Old Testament story

Most Common English Order of Old Testament Books	Earliest Attested Hebrew Order of Old Testament Books[5]
PART 1: THE PENTATEUCH	**PART 1: THE LAW (TORAH)**
Genesis	Genesis
Exodus	Exodus
Leviticus	Leviticus
Numbers	Numbers
Deuteronomy	Deuteronomy
PART 2: THE HISTORICAL BOOKS	**PART 2: THE PROPHETS (NEVI'IM)**
Joshua	*Joshua*
Judges	*Judges*
Ruth	*1–2 Samuel*
1–2 Samuel	*1–2 Kings*
1–2 Kings	Jeremiah
1–2 Chronicles	Ezekiel
Ezra	Isaiah
Nehemiah	The Book of the Twelve: Hosea, Joel, Amos, Obadiah, Jonah, Micah, Nahum, Habakkuk, Zephaniah, Haggai, Zechariah, Malachi
Esther	**PART 3: THE WRITINGS (KETUVIM)**
PART 3: THE POETIC BOOKS	*Ruth*
Job	Psalms
Psalms	Job
Proverbs	Proverbs
Ecclesiastes	Ecclesiastes
Song of Songs	Song of Songs
PART 4: THE PROPHETS	Lamentations
Isaiah	Daniel
Jeremiah	*Esther*
Lamentations	*Ezra–Nehemiah*
Ezekiel	*1–2 Chronicles*
Daniel	
The Twelve Minor Prophets: Hosea, Joel, Amos, Obadiah, Jonah, Micah, Nahum, Habakkuk, Zephaniah, Haggai, Zechariah, Malachi	

[5]This order is articulated in *Baba Bathra* 14b. *Baba Bathra* was written in AD 200, but its tradition possibly goes back as far as 150 BC. See Stephen G. Dempster, "A Wandering Moabite: Ruth—A Book in Search of a Canonical Home," in *The Shape of the Writings*, ed. Julius Steinberg and Timothy J. Stone, Siphrut 16 (Eisenbrauns, 2015), 94–95, following Roger Beckwith, *The Old Testament Canon of the New Testament Church and Its Background in Early Judaism* (Eerdmans, 1986).

Although much more could be said on this topic, a few simple observations will lead us to some unexpected insights.[6] Our English Bibles divide the Old Testament into four sections: Pentateuch, Historical Books, Poetic Books, and Prophets. In contrast, the Hebrew Old Testament is divided into three sections: Law, Prophets, and Writings.

As we scan table I.1 for the books in italics—the books that unfold the Old Testament story of redemption beyond the Pentateuch—we discover a major difference in order. While our English Bibles most often group these books together, as Historical Books, the earliest attested Hebrew order places half of them at the beginning of the Prophets section, half of them at the end of the Writings section, and one of them in between. Since most Christian readers will be familiar with the order found in the English Bible, it may at first seem logical to follow this order as we unfold the Old Testament story. To challenge this assumption, let's turn to the New Testament.

The order of Old Testament books according to the New Testament. At the end of Luke's Gospel, the risen Jesus reveals himself to a group of his followers and teaches them from the Old Testament:

> Then he said to them, "These are my words that I spoke to you while I was still with you, that *everything written about me in the Law of Moses and the Prophets and the Psalms must be fulfilled*." Then he opened their minds to understand the Scriptures, and said to them, "Thus it

[6]This is an extremely complicated topic. To dig deeper, see Jason S. DeRouchie, "The Hermeneutical Significance of the Shape of the Christian Canon," in *The Law, the Prophets, and the Writings: Studies in Evangelical Old Testament Hermeneutics in Honor of Duane A. Garrett*, ed. Andrew M. King et al. (B&H Academic, 2021), 29-56; Alex Duke et al., "On Opening Up Your Mind to Something You've Never Considered—Or, the Weirdest Episode of Bible Talk Yet," *Bible Talk* (podcast), May 3, 2023, www.9marks.org/conversations/on-opening-up-your-mind-to-something-youve-never-considered-or-the-weirdest-episode-of-bible-talk-yet-bible-talk-ep-82/. Prior to the invention of physical books as we know them, the order of Old Testament books was represented in ancient lists of canonical books. It would have also been preserved by placing scrolls in ordered niches on a wall in the Jerusalem temple—the ancient version of bookshelves. See Stephen G. Dempster, "A Wandering Moabite: Ruth—A Book in Search of a Canonical Home," in *The Shape of the Writings*, ed. Julius Steinberg and Timothy J. Stone, Siphrut 16 (Eisenbrauns, 2015), 98.

> is written, that the Christ should suffer and on the third day rise from the dead, and that repentance for the forgiveness of sins should be proclaimed in his name to all nations, beginning from Jerusalem." (Lk 24:44-47, emphasis added)

In this scene, Jesus focuses on the heart of the gospel (Lk 24:46-47). Less clear for most Christians is where Jesus found these truths: "in the Law of Moses and the Prophets and the Psalms" (Lk 24:44). If we assume the English order of Old Testament books with its four sections, this verse is puzzling. But as we turn to table I.1 again, the answer is clear: Jesus thought in terms of a Hebrew Old Testament order, with *three sections*: "in the Law of Moses and the Prophets and the Psalms" (with the Psalms as the first main book in—and probable early title for—the third section, later called "the Writings").[7] This suggests that Jesus (and Luke) thought of an Old Testament in three sections—Law, Prophets, and Writings. In fact, as we read the entire New Testament with this question in mind, we discover many other examples, often with "the Law and the Prophets" as yet another shorthand way of referring to the entire Old Testament.[8]

Next, we turn to the Gospel of Matthew. In this scene Jesus is pronouncing woes on the scribes and Pharisees because they killed, crucified, flogged, and persecuted the faithful prophets God sent to them. He continues, "so that on you may come all the righteous blood shed on earth, from the blood of righteous Abel to the blood of Zechariah

---

[7]In the Hebrew way of thinking, one way to title something is to name its first part. For example, the Hebrew name of the book of Genesis is "In the beginning"—the first few words (actually, it is one word in Hebrew) of the book.

[8]Gallagher and Meade note that a previous generation of scholars typically understood "the Law and the Prophets" to refer to the first two sections of the Hebrew Old Testament, but that most scholars now believe this is shorthand for the entire Old Testament. See Edmon L. Gallagher and John D. Meade, *The Biblical Canon Lists from Early Christianity: Texts and Analysis* (Oxford University Press, 2017), 8. Thanks to Jonny Atkinson for pointing me to this quotation (personal correspondence). To cite only two examples of many, in a conversation in Acts 24:14, the apostle Paul refers to the Law and the Prophets. Also, in Rom 3:21, Paul writes that the Law and the Prophets bear witness to the righteousness of God.

the son of Barachiah, whom you murdered between the sanctuary and the altar" (Mt 23:35). This heavy passage is filled with practical teaching, and it also attests to the order of Old Testament books according to Jesus. Since Abel was the first murder victim in the Old Testament (see Gen 4) and Zechariah was the last (according to the Hebrew order; see 2 Chron 24:20-22), the implication is that Jesus worked with an Old Testament that began with Genesis and ended with Chronicles.[9]

The Hebrew order of Old Testament books affects our theology. It seems clear that Jesus and the New Testament authors thought in terms of a Hebrew order of Old Testament books, but does this matter? In this case, yes, because the order of books affects the way we experience the Bible's unfolding story of redemption.

When Steve Jobs was getting ready to launch the iTunes Store, he had to negotiate with the record labels to be able to sell their songs individually. Previous to this, if consumers wanted one song, they needed to purchase an entire album. As word spread to the musicians about these negotiations, many were up in arms. They argued that they did write individual songs but they also took care to shape them into albums. The songs were meant to fit together and to be heard in relation to one another *in the order the artists had laid out*. In the end, Jobs (and Apple) won, and the artists were left feeling like something was lost.[10]

Something similar is true of the Old Testament: As we unfold its redemption story in the earliest attested Hebrew order, we discover many fresh insights. While our English Bibles are ordered in terms of *genre*, with chronology as a second consideration, the Hebrew Old Testament is shaped with a primary emphasis on *theme*, with both

[9]For a helpful summary of views on the identity of Zechariah the son of Barachiah, see D. A. Carson, "Matthew," in *Matthew, Mark, Luke*, ed. Temper Longman III and David E. Garland, The Expositor's Bible Commentary 9 (Zondervan Academic, 1984), 485-86n35. Thanks to Daniel Bredin for pointing me to this source (personal correspondence).

[10]See Walter Isaacson, *Steve Jobs* (Simon & Schuster, 2021), 397.

genre and chronology as significant but occasionally secondary when such an ordering best serves the thematic flow of the story.[11]

Although we'll dig deeper in the following chapters, let's whet our appetites for some of the insights that will spring from reading the Old Testament in this order. In chapter six we will marvel at the in-grafting of a Moabite named Ruth into the people of God—*even with King David in her lineage.* According to the earliest attested Hebrew order, the messianic hope in the Psalms and the rest of the Writings is to be read through the lens of its preface, the book of Ruth. As I will explain more fully, this hints at a coming Savior in the family of David (see 2 Sam 7:16) whose work will affect not just Jews but the entire world (see Gen 12:1-3).[12]

We will also discover why the Hebrew Old Testament concludes out of chronological order, with Ezra–Nehemiah preceding Chronicles. As I will explain more in chapters eight and nine, this results in a forward-looking, hope-filled conclusion to the Old Testament—of an ultimate return from exile, with a king in David's lineage reigning forever (see 2 Sam 7:16) and YHWH dwelling among his people in a manner that will be bigger and better than they had ever experienced. As the Old Testament leaves us yearning for this fullness, it will be richly achieved in part three of the Bible's redemption story—its climax in the Lord Jesus.

THE PATH AHEAD

Now that we have been oriented to the second act of the Bible's redemption story, we will spend nine chapters discovering its major themes. In the chapters that follow, we will begin with the land as a settled home for the redeemed before considering the judges as those

---

[11]I first learned these helpful distinctions from Miles Van Pelt's lectures on Old Testament biblical theology. See Craig Blomberg et al., *A Guide to Biblical Theology*, n.d., www.biblicaltraining.org/learn/academy/bt201-a-guide-to-biblical-theology. Our English Bibles reflect the order of the Greek translation of the Old Testament from the few hundred years leading up to Christ.

[12]See Dempster, "Wandering Moabite," 100.

who delivered the redeemed. We'll look at the Old Testament kings as covenant heads who led and represented the redeemed and the prophets as figures who proclaimed the word of YHWH to the redeemed. We'll stand in horror as the story unfolds in division, decline, and exile—tragedy for the redeemed. We'll see the theme of ingrafting as YHWH's means of extending the redeemed and the theme of sojourning as YHWH preserving his redeemed while they are in exile. Finally, in the return and rebuilding we will notice a partly accomplished second redemption before the story ends with forward-looking hope: of an ultimate redemption that will be fully accomplished. Along the way, we will close each chapter by looking forward to Christ, concluding with discussion questions to help us further exult in him, either with a group or on our own.

LOOKING FORWARD TO CHRIST: A TWO-YEAR LECTURE SERIES ON JESUS FROM THE OLD TESTAMENT

I have been making the claim that the Old Testament story should lead us to Christ. Before I conclude this introduction, let's look at one more example.

We have noticed a sampling of Jesus' claims that the Old Testament is filled with gospel treasures. As we turn to the book of Acts, we discover that Jesus was not alone in this assertion. By the end of Acts the apostle Paul was in prison after experiencing a long and fruitful ministry throughout the known world of his day. Still, he longed to go to Rome to testify about Jesus. In Acts 28 he finally got there through a prison transfer. Even in these difficult circumstances, Paul still yearned to preach Christ.

When he arrived in Rome, the local Christians visited him with greetings, and this encouraged Paul. He wasn't a threat, so he was allowed to stay by himself with a soldier to guard him. This allowed Paul to call together the local leaders of the Jews. They came—likely out of curiosity—and he immediately claimed that nothing he had said or done was out of step with the Old Testament. In fact, he claimed that it was because of the hope of Israel that he was wearing chains. In response, they invited him to speak; they had heard *about* Christianity, but now they could hear a clear explanation directly from a prominent Christian who had been trained as a Jewish rabbi.

The scene unfolds: "When they had appointed a day for him, they came to him at his lodging in greater numbers. From morning till evening he expounded to them, testifying to the kingdom of God and trying to convince them about Jesus both from the Law of Moses and from the Prophets" (Acts 28:23). This was a sermon that lasted from morning until evening. But those in attendance didn't complain because what they heard was compelling and they wanted to consider it carefully. Did you notice the topic of Paul's sermon? He testifies to the kingdom of God and seeks to convince the people about Jesus. And did you notice the text he preaches from? The Law of Moses and the Prophets. Now that we have learned the structure of the Old Testament in its Hebrew order, we know what this means. There is so much about the kingdom of God and Jesus on every page of the Old Testament that Paul could fill an entire day of preaching.[13]

But there is more. At the end of the scene, we read that Paul "lived there *two whole years* at his own expense, and welcomed all who came to him, proclaiming the kingdom of God and teaching about the Lord Jesus Christ with all boldness and without hindrance" (Acts 28:30-31, emphasis added). These are the last two verses of Acts, and the very last word of the book (in the original Greek) translates into English as "without hindrance." Paul was in prison, Christians were being persecuted, but the word of God went forth boldly and without hindrance—and it continues to do so today. Notice also that the theme of Paul's preaching has not changed—he proclaims the kingdom of

[13]It is likely that because the third section of the Old Testament had not yet been named "the Writings," "the Law and the Prophets" served as shorthand for the entire Old Testament. For a more in-depth explanation, see n8 on p. 11.

God and teaches about the Lord Jesus Christ. From earlier in this scene we know that his habit was to teach these things from the Law of Moses and the Prophets. But this time, how long did Paul's teaching last? *Two whole years.*

There is a richness in the Old Testament, and we miss it when we complain about our encounter with a boring record of land allotment, an even more boring nine-chapter genealogy, a disturbing scene of holy war, or a repulsive story of a Levite and his concubine. I am not suggesting that we should *enjoy* the gruesome details. I am suggesting that according to Jesus and Paul and all the New Testament authors, we should be pointed to Christ from every part of the Old Testament. If we wake up in the morning and read the Old Testament and we don't walk away with gospel nourishment, we are not reading the Old Testament like Jesus or Paul. If we hear a sermon (or preach a sermon) from the Old Testament that doesn't have the good news of Jesus as its climax, we are not hearing (or preaching) the Old Testament the way it was meant to be heard (or proclaimed). We are meant to be pointed to Christ.

When we encounter the Old Testament and are not pointed to Christ, the problem is not with the Old Testament. The problem is with us. Sometimes my doctor sits me down with my legs hanging from the side of his examination table. He pulls out a (rubber) reflex hammer and lightly taps my knee. Whether I want to or not, I kick. In the chapters that follow, we will seek to grow our knee-jerk reaction to be pointed to Jesus and the gospel from every page of the Old Testament. But before we dive in, let's dig into some questions that will help us digest what we have learned so far.

DISCUSSION QUESTIONS

1. Why did a miraculous healing in John 5 turn into a debate about the Old Testament?

2. As you read about some of the challenges in applying the unfolding Old Testament story to life in the twenty-first century, which ones resonated most with you? Can you think of others that are also a challenge?
3. How do Deuteronomy 28; 30:1-10 act as a lens for reading the unfolding Old Testament story beyond the Pentateuch?
4. Survey your group: Have you ever heard that the order of books in most English translations of the Old Testament differs from the earliest attested Hebrew order?
5. Which New Testament passages support reading the Old Testament in its Hebrew order—with three sections and with Chronicles last?
6. In this chapter, it was argued that the order in which we read the Old Testament books affects our theology. Were any of the initial examples compelling, or are you still unsure about this claim? Share some specific examples to support your answer.
7. In this chapter, we looked at John 5:39; Luke 24:44-47; and Acts 28:17-31 as New Testament evidence that we are meant to read the Old Testament and be pointed to Christ. Did the chapter draw anything out from these passages you had not noticed before? Share with your group.

LAND

SETTLING THE REDEEMED

If we find the book of Joshua challenging, we are not alone. This book is focused on Israel's offensive military takeover of the land of Canaan. In some battles YHWH calls his people to eradicate everything that breathes, including women, children, and livestock. At other times survivors are allowed, including a Canaanite prostitute and her family during one battle, and an entire people group in another. As the battle scenes taper off, the book gets geographical, with nine relentless chapters of ancient place names and tribal allotments.

Although our initial impression of Joshua may be lukewarm, its inclusion in God's Word should lead us to search for answers to the parts of the book we find challenging. As we understand the book of Joshua in the flow of the Bible's grand story of redemption, we discover a message that is extremely encouraging, practical, and life-giving. In this chapter, we will dive into the surprisingly important theme of a land for God's people. We'll begin in the books that lead into Joshua, and this will equip us to understand the book of Joshua in a much deeper way. We'll close with some wonderful gospel applications as we look forward in the Bible's story to the way Jesus fulfills the Old Testament hope.

GENESIS 1–3: THE LAND CREATED, GIFTED, LOST, AND ANTICIPATED

Before we can make sense of a land for Israel in the book of Joshua, we need a big-picture understanding of the Old Testament teaching on this theme. The Hebrew word *erets* is translated "earth" or "land," depending on its wider context. This word appears 2,504 times over the 929 chapters of the Old Testament, including its first and last verses (Gen 1:1; 2 Chron 36:23). That is an average of more than two and a half times per chapter.[1] But this is not all: The Hebrew word *adamah* is translated "ground," "land," or "earth," depending on its wider context, and it appears 222 times in the Old Testament—from Genesis 1:25 to 2 Chronicles 33:8. This reveals that from beginning to end, the Old Testament tells a very earthy story of redemption.

In Genesis 2, the camera lens zooms in, with an intimate look at the creation of the man and the woman. In this scene, YHWH God plants a garden—more earthiness—where he puts the man to work it and keep it (Gen 2:8, 15). Then he creates the woman and performs the first marriage ceremony (Gen 2:18, 21-25). In the original creation, place matters: Eden is an enclosed, protected sanctuary, where YHWH God walks among his people in perfect fellowship (Gen 3:8).

Then paradise is lost. Genesis 3 tells the tragic story of temptation by the serpent and the first couple's rebellion against God's word. Although they have been lavished with every imaginable blessing, they grasp for more, and so they lose it all. At this time they are cast out of the special land where YHWH God dwelled in their midst (Gen 3:22-24).

I have a calendar in my home that features the art of Thomas Kinkade. In it, Kinkade explains the rationale for his *Hometown Lake* painting: "I believe that people in every area of our nation and all parts of our culture share this vision, this longing for a peaceful

[1]This is not to say that *erets* occurs in every chapter. It does not. But it is the sixth-most frequently occurring noun in the Hebrew Old Testament.

lakeside place."[2] Genesis 3 not only makes sense of this longing for a peaceful lakeside place; it also reveals why such a haven will never ultimately satisfy our deepest longings. Even for those who have been reconciled to God through Christ, Hometown Lake is still affected by the fall into sin. Mosquitos still bite. Weeds still grow. Hot summers and cold winters are still unbearable. And disease and death still make Hometown Lake a place of pain and tragic loss.

Genesis 3 explains why we yearn for a real, earthy haven, one that is much more satisfying than Hometown Lake. And it also begins to paint a glorious portrait of redemption that will unfold for the rest of the Bible's story. Even as our first parents were about to be barred from their perfect garden sanctuary, YHWH God promised that a descendant of the woman would one day win the ultimate victory over the descendant of the serpent (Gen 3:15). And as another initial act of kindness, YHWH God covered the shame of his people (Gen 3:21). Even before he cast humanity out of the garden, YHWH God was already hinting toward an eventual restoration.[3]

THE REST OF THE PENTATEUCH: THE PROMISE OF LAND

The rest of Genesis unfolds east of Eden, outside YHWH's special earthy place. Along the way, the story builds on the promise that YHWH will redeem a people for himself and that he will also open the way to a real, earthy place where he will live among those people once again.

This theme is prominent at the call of Abram, when YHWH commands, "Go *from your country* and your kindred and your father's house *to the land that I will show you*" (Gen 12:1, emphasis added). Once again, place matters. Abram obeys, and when he arrives, YHWH promises that he will give that very land to Abram's offspring (Gen 12:7). Then Abram travels through the land of Canaan, building

[2]Thomas Kinkade, *Thomas Kinkade Special Collector's Edition 2024 Deluxe Wall Calendar with Print: Lakeside Splendor* (Andrews McMeel, 2023).

[3]For this reason, Sandra L. Richter describes the Bible's big-picture story as the epic of Eden. See Sandra L. Richter, *The Epic of Eden: A Christian Entry into the Old Testament* (IVP Academic, 2008).

altars to YHWH (Gen 12:7-8). By doing this he is claiming the land for YHWH—this is a geographical locale where YHWH will be worshiped. The Canaanites may have possessed it at the time, but Abram believed YHWH's promise.

As the book of Genesis unfolds, the land promise to Abram is filled out with more details. For example, YHWH speaks of the expansiveness of the land that will be an everlasting possession for his offspring (Gen 13:14-15; 17:8). YHWH will multiply Abraham's offspring "as the stars of heaven and as the sand that is on the seashore," and Abraham's offspring will "possess the gate of his enemies" (Gen 22:17). Later, YHWH promises Abraham's son, "To your offspring I will give *all these lands*" (Gen 26:3, emphasis added). When Genesis 22:17 and Genesis 26:3 are read together, they reveal that Abraham's descendants will be innumerable, and they will also possess "the gate of his enemies" and "all these lands" (Gen 22:17; 26:3).[4] These passages hint that the borders of this Promised Land will begin small and eventually grow to accommodate an expanding people of God.

Despite the amazing promise of YHWH, Abraham never enjoys its earthy fullness. In fact, YHWH tells him his descendants will have to wait four hundred years until this promise will be fulfilled (Gen 15:13-16). In his lifetime, Abraham owns only a tiny gravesite in Canaan (Gen 23). But this gravesite for Sarah (and later Abraham) is purchased in faith that YHWH will one day fulfill his earthy promises. For this reason, when Abraham's grandson Jacob dies in Egypt, he arranges for his remains to be carried to this same grave (Gen 50:4-14). Then, in the exodus from Egypt, the bones of Joseph are also transferred from Egypt to the grave in Canaan that Abraham purchased (Ex 13:19).

The exodus is an exit out of Egypt and toward the land of Canaan, where God's people will dwell with him (e.g., Ex 3:8). But when they sin by worshiping a golden calf, YHWH says he will *not* go with his

---

[4]I was first pointed to the connection between Gen 22:17 and Gen 26:3 in Oren Martin, *Bound for the Promised Land*, New Studies in Biblical Theology 34 (IVP Academic, 2015), 71-73.

people into the Promised Land (Ex 33:3). Moses replies with a desperate prayer of intercession: "If your presence will not go with me, do not bring us up from here. For how shall it be known that I have found favor in your sight, I and your people? Is it not in your going with us, so that we are distinct, I and your people, from every other people on the face of the earth?" (Ex 33:15-16). In the end, YHWH relents and agrees to accompany his people into the Promised Land.

What does Exodus 33 teach us? The Promised Land was not to be an ancient Near Eastern version of Thomas Kinkade's Hometown Lake. If it were to be a beautiful, serene place without the special presence of YHWH among his special, redeemed people, it would be an empty shell. YHWH's promise of a land was not merely so that his people could finally settle into family homes with pastoral views. The reason the Promised Land would be a blessing was clear: YHWH would be there, and his people would experience settledness and rest in his presence and under his favor. From this place they could worship YHWH freely and fulfill their role as a kingdom of priests who would shine the light of YHWH to the nations around them (see Ex 19:6). For these reasons, Israel's settledness in the land would be another step in the Bible's story toward a return to Eden.

Later, YHWH initiates the fulfillment of his promise, when he sends spies to scout out the land before his people take it in battle (Num 13:1-2). But the people respond with fear, and their unbelief means that an entire generation has to die during a forty-year hiatus in the wilderness.

Later still, Deuteronomy finds the next generation of God's people perched on the border of the Promised Land. In three long speeches, Moses prepares them to enter. These include the promise of blessings for covenant keeping, curses for covenant breaking, and restoration for covenant repentance (Deut 28; 30:1-10; cf. Lev 26). A central feature of these warnings is the people's proximity to the land: If they keep the covenant, they will be blessed in the land; if they break the covenant, they will be driven from the land; if they repent from their sin, they will be restored to the land.

JOSHUA: ENTERING AND POSSESSING THE LAND

In light of what we have learned in the story so far, the tremendous blessing of a land for God's people comes into focus. Far more significant than a people group's desire to have a settled place to call their own, the Promised Land was a spiritual blessing from Israel's covenant God. In this place, other gods would not be worshiped, YHWH would dwell among his people, and they would be free to worship him in the way he commanded. To use the language of the Bible, they would be given *rest*. As we will see, Israel's possession of the land in Joshua would not usher in the ultimate, promised rest, but it would be a significant step toward this goal.

The book of Joshua has four big sections, and James M. Hamilton Jr. has pointed out that each part is best understood when we notice its key, repeated word.[5] As we embark on the book, table 1.1 expands on Hamilton's breakdown:

Table 1.1. The unfolding story of Joshua

Section of Joshua	Key Word	Example Scripture Passage
Joshua 1–5	"crossing over" into the land (also translated "passing over," "passing through," etc.)	And Joshua commanded the officers of the people, "*Pass through* the midst of the camp and command the people, 'Prepare your provisions, for within three days you are to *pass over* this Jordan to go in to take possession of the land that the LORD your God is giving you to possess.'" (Josh 1:10-11, emphasis added)
Joshua 6–12	"taking" the land (in battle)	"Joshua *took* all that land, the hill country and all the Negeb and all the land of Goshen and the lowland and the Arabah and the hill country of Israel and its lowland." (Josh 11:16, emphasis added)

[5]See James M. Hamilton Jr., *God's Glory in Salvation Through Judgment: A Biblical Theology* (Crossway, 2010), 144. For a similar reckoning, see also Stephen G. Dempster, *Dominion and Dynasty: A Theology of the Hebrew Bible*, New Studies in Biblical Theology 15 (InterVarsity Press, 2003), 126-27.

Section of Joshua	Key Word	Example Scripture Passage
Joshua 13–21	"apportioning" the land to each tribe of Israel (also translated "allotting" or "dividing")	"The people of Israel did as the LORD commanded Moses; they *allotted* the land." (Josh 14:5, emphasis added)
Joshua 22–24	"serving" YHWH in the land (and *not* "serving" foreign gods)	"Now therefore fear the LORD and *serve* him in sincerity and in faithfulness. Put away the gods that your fathers *served* beyond the River and in Egypt, and *serve* the LORD." (Josh 24:14, emphasis added)

Joshua 1–5: Crossing over into the land. Deuteronomy concludes with Israel on the cusp of entering the Promised Land, and in Joshua 1–5, the Hebrew word for "crossing over" is emphasized.[6] In this section, Israel finally moves into the land YHWH promised to Abraham's descendants. The book famously begins with repeated calls for Joshua and the people to "be strong and courageous," but in context this is much more than a pep talk about personal strength and courage. YHWH promised Israel this land, and YHWH is about to give it to them. Strength and courage will be rooted in trusting YHWH and his word. As YHWH puts it, "Only be strong and very courageous, being careful to do according to all the law that Moses my servant commanded you. Do not turn from it to the right hand or to the left, that you may have good success wherever you go" (Josh 1:7).

In Joshua 1–5 Israel keeps YHWH's torah, or instruction, as they send spies into the land, cross over into the land, circumcise the new generation of males, and celebrate the Passover in Canaan. In particular, the story of Israel crossing over into the land is told in a similar way to the Red Sea crossing of the exodus: In both scenes YHWH causes the waters—this time, of the Jordan River—to stop up so Israel can pass through on dry ground (Josh 3). This is a signal to the people that YHWH will be with them in this crossing over into the Promised

---

[6]Also translated as "go over," "pass over," "went through," etc.

Land, just as he was with the previous generation of his people in the exodus from Egypt.

Joshua 6–12: Taking the land. Next, Joshua 6–12 describes Israel taking the land through a series of battles. From the outset, YHWH's blessing on these endeavors is clear, as a Canaanite prostitute named Rahab believes that YHWH is going to give Israel success in battle. She houses and hides the spies in her home in Jericho, and then sends them away with an escape plan (Josh 2). For this reason, this most unlikely of converts is incorporated into Israel at the end of the battle with Jericho (Josh 6). What a wonderful display of YHWH's blessing to all the people of the earth (Gen 12:3). In this first battle, YHWH also disables Jericho's defenses, but only as his people obey his strict marching orders. After the walls of the city are destroyed by YHWH, the people enter and win the battle.

This scene raises two ethical questions that surface numerous times in Joshua: Why did YHWH sanction a war of aggression, and why did YHWH command his people to devote everything in the city to destruction? As we begin to think through these questions, we should guard against making light of their gravity. I freely acknowledge we won't be able to resolve all the tensions in a chapter as brief as this one, nor should we ever make light of any biblical scene in which YHWH pours out his wrath. But what we will be able to see is how the events in this book are important for the Bible's understanding of God and his unfolding plan of redemption. What are some insights to help us make sense of this unique event from biblical history?

The first challenge is answered when we look all the way back in the biblical story to Genesis 15. In this chapter, YHWH initiates his covenant with Abram. This passage reveals that Abram's descendants will be servants in a foreign land for four hundred years and that YHWH will then judge the nation they serve and bring them out with great possessions (Gen 15:13-14). Four hundred years before the exodus from Egypt, YHWH predicted it to Abram. The reason for this four-hundred-year wait is also revealed: "For the iniquity of the Amorites is not yet complete" (Gen 15:16).

Gordon Wenham explains that in Genesis 15:16, "the Amorites stand for all the inhabitants of Canaan" who lived there prior to Israel.[7] Although we are not told the specific sin of the Amorites in this verse, 1 Kings 21:26 reveals that the later King Ahab "acted very abominably in going after idols, *as the Amorites had done*, whom the LORD cast out before the people of Israel" (emphasis added). In this verse, the idolatry of the Amorites is said to be the reason they were cast out of the land in the book of Joshua. Brian Rosner explains why this was the case: "In the Bible there is no more serious charge than that of idolatry. Idolatry called for the strictest punishment, elicited the most disdainful polemic, prompted the most extreme measures of avoidance, and was regarded as the chief identifying characteristic of those who were the very antithesis of the people of God, namely, the Gentiles."[8] This is because YHWH is the only true God and therefore is rightly jealous for all worship to be reserved for him alone (e.g., Ex 20:5).[9]

The Hoover Dam is a wonder of early twentieth-century engineering. It is fed by the Colorado River, fills Lake Meade, and at capacity can "contain 28.9 million acre-feet of water covering about 248 square miles."[10] Imagine for a moment that a reservoir of this size was dry but was slowly being refilled by a garden hose. In this illustration, the massive, empty reservoir represents the extent of YHWH's patience and mercy, and the water trickling in represents his wrath, prompted by humanity's sin. The four-hundred-year wait until

---

[7]Gordon J. Wenham, *Genesis 1–15*, Word Biblical Commentary (Zondervan, 1987), 332. See also Victor P. Hamilton, *The Book of Genesis: Chapters 1–17*, New International Commentary on the Old Testament (Eerdmans, 1990), 436.

[8]Brian S. Rosner, "Idolatry," in *New Dictionary of Biblical Theology*, ed. T. Desmond Alexander and Brian S. Rosner (InterVarsity Press, 2000), 570.

[9]While at first it may sound counterintuitive to think of God's jealousy as a positive thing, consider that he is the only being in the universe for whom jealousy is *not* a sin, since he truly *is* God and so truly *does* deserve all worship, commitment, and devotion.

[10]"Hoover Dam," Water Education Foundation, n.d., www.watereducation.org/aquapedia/hoover-dam.

Abram's descendants can possess Canaan is precisely because YHWH is "a God merciful and gracious, slow to anger, and abounding in steadfast love and faithfulness, keeping steadfast love for thousands, forgiving iniquity and transgression and sin" (Ex 34:6-7). But during those four hundred years, the sin of the Amorite people will cause YHWH's wrath to keep trickling into the dam until it will finally overflow and burst forth. This is because YHWH is also a God "who will by no means clear the guilty" (Ex 34:7).

This means that the wars in the book of Joshua are not mainly political wars of aggression. In these wars, YHWH is *simultaneously* giving Israel the land he promised them and using Israel as his means of pouring out his wrath on a people group's long-standing lifestyle of iniquity. As Stephen G. Dempster puts it, "The coming of the kingdom means that Israel must be agents of divine judgment, purging the land of its sinful population, preparing it for the presence of the holiness of God."[11] Since the lives of their enemies—which were given by God—are being used to destroy God's image and corrupt God's world, they are offered back to God in an act of divine judgment.[12]

David J. H. Beldman adds, "The conquest of Canaan was a one-time event in the history of God's plan of salvation. The conquest was indeed commanded by God, but it was a unique event with a limited scope. Conquest was not a pattern that Yahweh set for his people; their identity was not as a conquering nation."[13] The trickle of YHWH's wrath prompted by this people's sin had filled the massive reservoir of YHWH's patience beyond capacity, and so the dam of YHWH's wrath burst forth, and Israel was the vessel of that wrath.

As a Canaanite prostitute named Rahab is spared and, along with her family, incorporated into Israel, we learn that even at the eleventh

[11]Stephen G. Dempster, *The Return of the Kingdom: A Biblical Theology of God's Reign* (IVP Academic, 2024), 100.

[12]See Dempster, *Return of the Kingdom*, 107.

[13]David J. H. Beldman, *Deserting the King: The Book of Judges*, Transformative Word (Lexham, 2017), 76.

hour, if any of those great sinners would come to YHWH's side, they would be rescued and incorporated into his people. And since the Israelite Achan will later be put to death by YHWH for his sin (Josh 7), we learn that YHWH's distribution of judgment or mercy has nothing to do with ethnicity, gender, or any other arbitrary thing: The issue is faithfulness or unfaithfulness to YHWH.[14]

This also helps to explain the other ethical challenge in Joshua: the slaughter of seemingly innocent civilians and the destruction of property (including livestock). YHWH had already made clear to Israel through Moses that all the nations that currently inhabited Canaan had polluted the land with wicked practices.[15] He had also commanded that these wicked nations be devoted to complete destruction in order to keep idolaters and idolatry out of Israel's home with YHWH.[16] Paul R. House adds further, "Israel's role as instrument of divine punishment is accentuated by its commitment to take no spoil but rather to place all captured wealth in the treasury of the Lord (6:18-19). This is not an excursion meant to enhance Israel's financial standing."[17]

As we step back and survey the Bible's big-picture story, we also discover that the holy wars in Joshua are not the Bible's greatest display of God's wrath. These wars pale in comparison to the great white throne judgment described in Revelation 20. On this great and terrible day, judgment will not merely come for individuals or cities or even for all people living at a specific time in history. Every person who has ever lived will be raised for judgment. They will stand before the great white throne and will either gloriously enter a new heaven and a new earth in God's presence forever (Rev 21–22) or they will be thrown into the lake of fire (Rev 20:15), a place where "their worm

---

[14]I first learned this insight in Andreas J. Köstenberger and Gregory Goswell, *Biblical Theology: A Canonical, Thematic, and Ethical Approach* (Crossway, 2023), 165-66.

[15]See, e.g., Lev 18, especially Lev 18:24-25, 27.

[16]See Deut 7, especially Deut 7:2, 5, 25. This point is also made in Deut 20:10-18.

[17]Paul R. House, *Old Testament Theology* (InterVarsity Press, 1998), 204.

shall not die, their fire shall not be quenched, and they shall be an abhorrence to all flesh" (Is 66:24; cf. Mk 9:48). The wars in Joshua are a sober display of YHWH's just wrath toward unrepentant sinners, but they ultimately point forward in the Bible's story to the final judgment for all people of all time.

Joshua 13–21: Apportioning the land. After the holy wars, the apportioning of the land comes in Joshua 13–21. To twenty-first-century readers, these chapters are likely difficult to enjoy because they are a detailed record of geographical boundaries, place names, and land lotteries. For the ancient Israelite reader, though, every detail in these chapters was glorious.

If any of us were to receive a vast inheritance, would we be *bored* as the lawyer read through every detail about every investment and every property that was now ours? To the heir, the lawyer could read all day, and their excitement would only grow. Since the land allotment in the book of Joshua was much more than a *physical* inheritance, its possession was even more glorious. This land was a gift from YHWH, a place for his people to own and into which they would settle. Most importantly, it was the location where YHWH would settle *among* his redeemed people, where they would be free to worship him in the way he commanded. These chapters are a crucial step toward the Bible's ultimate goal of YHWH's people entering a new and better garden of Eden, a return to YHWH's presence and favor that will never be lost and will only be glorious.

Joshua 18:1 is a great summary verse for this section: "Then the whole congregation of the people of Israel assembled at Shiloh and set up the tent of meeting there. The land lay subdued before them." Oren Martin explains the important link between rest in the land and tabernacle: "The dwelling place of God is set up *after* rest has been achieved."[18] Once again, YHWH's gift of land has a purpose: so

[18]Martin, *Bound for the Promised Land*, 89.

YHWH can dwell in the midst of his people (in the tabernacle), and his people can freely worship him in the way he commands.

In case we are tempted to look back on this section of Joshua as the highest point in the Bible's story, these chapters also hint toward something ominous. Although Joshua emphasizes the faithfulness of YHWH in lavishing his people with their inheritance, we also discover whispers of trouble along the way, whispers that will turn to shouts in the book of Judges. While Israel has clearly been called to rid the land of idolatry and to only ever follow YHWH's lead in battles, the Gibeonite people deceive Israel into making a covenant with them (Josh 9). Although they voluntarily become Israel's servants, Deuteronomy 7:2 was clear that making a covenant with Canaan's idolatrous inhabitants would pollute the land with continued idolatrous practices and tempt God's people to do the same. Hamilton explains further that the book adds short notes about Israel's failure to completely drive out "the Geshurites or the Maacathites (13:13), the Jebusites (15:63), or the Canaanites in Gezer (16:10), and a series of Canaanite cities remain in the allotment to Manasseh (17:11-13). Near the time of his death (23:14), Joshua warns Israel about the polluting influence of these wicked people (23:7, 12)."[19] Although the land is now under Israel's control, this control is not yet total.

Joshua 22–24: Serve YHWH in the land! Finally, in Joshua 22–24, the people are called to serve YHWH in the land (as opposed to serving other gods). The scene takes place many years after the allotment of land, near the end of Joshua's life. Joshua acknowledges the remaining peoples in the land and makes two speeches before he will die. In these, he calls the people to "do all that is written in the Book of the Law of Moses" and specifically not to "mix with these nations remaining among you or make mention of the names of their gods or swear by them or serve them or bow down to them" (Josh 23:6-7).

---

[19]Hamilton, *God's Glory in Salvation Through Judgment*, 152.

Instead, they are to "cling to the LORD your God just as you have done to this day" (Josh 23:8).

Joshua continues by warning Israel that if they cling to the nations that remained in the land, intermarrying with them and committing idolatry along with them, the nations will "be a snare and a trap for you, a whip on your sides and thorns in your eyes, until you perish from off this good ground that the LORD your God has given you" (Josh 23:13).

In his final speech, Joshua begins by reviewing YHWH's faithfulness from the promise to Abraham to the possession of the Promised Land (Josh 24:2-13). In light of this, he calls the people to choose that day whom they will serve: "But as for me and my house, we will serve the LORD" (Josh 24:15). The people respond with resolve, but Joshua's response is surprising: "You are not able to serve the LORD, for he is a holy God. He is a jealous God; he will not forgive your transgressions or your sins" (Josh 24:19). The book concludes with Joshua's death and a note that the people served YHWH during the days of Joshua and the elders who outlived him. Dempster observes, "The implication is that once these leaders were gone the people stopped following the Lord."[20] We'll have to wait until our next chapter to see this play out in the book of Judges.

LOOKING FORWARD TO CHRIST: ABRAHAM AND HIS OFFSPRING WILL BE HEIRS OF THE WORLD

We will fill out more of the Old Testament story of land in later chapters of this book. For now, it is enough to say in summary that the ominous warning at the end of Joshua will come to fruition: Israel will eventually lose their land. Although they will later return and rebuild under the leadership of Ezra and Nehemiah, this return will not be complete. The Old Testament concludes with a yearning for fullness.

[20]Dempster, *Dominion and Dynasty*, 130.

As we turn to the New Testament, we discover a primary emphasis on Christ's fulfillment of the Old Testament hope, the proclamation of the gospel, and the spread of the church to the ends of the earth. But far from merely *spiritualizing* the Old Testament promises of land, God will also lavish his people with an expansive (and eternal!) home. In the New Testament, the focus is primarily on forming his special people in Christ before the story climaxes with these people in their global, new-earthly inheritance.[21]

How should Christians apply the Old Testament land promises? As we read the New Testament with this question in mind, we discover that it develops a rich theology of the land in a focused, Christ-centered manner and also in an expansive, earthy manner.

A focused, Christ-centered view of the land. As we recall the main function of the land—that YHWH will settle among his settled people—we discover why the New Testament doesn't emphasize the land of Canaan as the geographical boundary of his people: Jesus *is* the presence of God dwelling intimately among his people. He is *Immanuel*, a Hebrew word that means "God with us" (Is 7:14; Mt 1:23). In fact, according to John's Gospel, Jesus is the Word who is eternal, who is with God, who is God, who is the Creator, and who is the source of life. *This Word* was made flesh and *tabernacled among us* (Jn 1:1-5, 14). Just like the first tabernacle, this tabernacle was fragile—Jesus was born in a human body with all of its weaknesses. Also just like the first tabernacle, this one also housed *the presence of God among us* (Jn 1:14). The Old Testament land, with YHWH dwelling among his people, pales in comparison to the focused, Christ-centered fulfillment of the land promises in the New Testament.

This also explains why Jesus can say, "Destroy this *temple*, and in three days I will raise it up," and why John can add, "He was speaking

[21]See Peter J. Gentry and Stephen J. Wellum, *Kingdom Through Covenant: A Biblical-Theological Understanding of the Covenants*, 2nd ed. (Crossway, 2018), 523; Martin, *Bound for the Promised Land*, 118.

about *the temple of his body*" (Jn 2:19, 21, emphasis added). Since the tabernacle and temple had the same purpose, the principle is the same. Here Jesus is talking about his coming death and resurrection on the third day. As he speaks to Jews in the Jerusalem temple, he also corrects them: The *real* temple, the temple to which the Old Testament temple pointed, *is his body.* Once again, in the person of Jesus, the land promises find their initial fulfillment because he *is* God's presence among his people.

An expansive, earthy view of the land. Earlier in this chapter, we noticed that the Old Testament does not define the geographical boundaries of the Promised Land with uniform precision. I suggested that this was to make room for an ever-expanding people of God who will possess "the gate of his enemies" and "all these lands" (Gen 22:17; 26:3). This seems to hint that the borders of the Promised Land will begin small and eventually grow to accommodate an ever-expanding people of God: Joshua 21:43-45 is just the beginning of Israel's possession of land.

Although Jesus embodies the purpose of the land, with God dwelling among his people, the New Testament also maintains the importance of place. In fact, it *expands* its borders. For example, in the Sermon on the Mount, Jesus promises that the meek will "inherit *the earth*" (Mt 5:5, emphasis added), and he also "taught his disciples to pray that God's (heavenly) kingdom would come to earth (Matt. 6:9-10)."[22] The apostle Paul later adds, "The promise to Abraham and his offspring that *he would be heir of the world* did not come through the law but through the righteousness of faith" (Rom 4:13, emphasis added). Jesus and Paul are clear: The Old Testament promise of land will not be ultimately fulfilled until God's people inherit *the entire world.*[23]

---

[22]Martin, *Bound for the Promised Land*, 126.

[23]In the Old Testament, Ps 72:8 and Zech 9:10 also speak of a coming king whose rule will be "from sea to sea, [and] from the River to the ends of the earth." Thanks to Jonny Atkinson for pointing me to these Old Testament texts (personal correspondence).

This explains why the most mature Christians live with a holy dissatisfaction: They yearn for a fullness that will never be completely attained in this life. Even though we have been redeemed by Christ and we are indwelled by the Holy Spirit, something much better is coming, and that something is *earthy*. As the apostle Peter teaches, "According to his promise we are waiting for new heavens and a new earth in which righteousness dwells" (2 Pet 3:13).

When a Christian dies, they are away from their body and at home with their Lord, which is better by far (2 Cor 5:8; Phil 1:23). But the Christian's *eternal* inheritance is *not* an out-of-body existence in heaven. There is something much better coming: a future when God's Old Testament people and New Testament believers in Jesus will be given eternal resurrection bodies that will never wear out. In those bodies, they will live on a new earth forever. In this awesome place it will be declared, "Behold, the dwelling place of God is with [humanity]. He will dwell with them, and they will be his people, and God himself will be with them as their God. He will wipe away every tear from their eyes, and death shall be no more, neither shall there be mourning, nor crying, nor pain anymore, for the former things have passed away" (Rev 21:3-4). The land promise for God's people is of an eternal, embodied, global inheritance.

Boyd Seevers summarizes beautifully the way Christians should apply the Old Testament land promises:

> When Christians read Joshua, every victory God secured and every claim of land Israel enjoyed should remind us of God's faithfulness and be viewed as a pointer to the great victory won by Jesus over the enemies of sin and death, which secured us a lasting inheritance (Col. 2:13-15; Heb. 2:14-15; 1 Peter 1:3-4). Those who read Joshua rightly, gain hope for the day when complete perfect peace will be realized throughout the entire world.[24]

---

[24]Boyd Seevers, "Joshua," in *What the Old Testament Authors Really Cared About: A Survey of Jesus' Bible*, ed. Jason S. DeRouchie (Kregel Academic, 2013), 174.

What a glorious day that will be! In the end, as we understand the Old Testament teaching on a land for God's people in light of the Bible's grand story, it deepens our love for Christ and helps us to yearn with certain hope for our future, awesome inheritance in a new heavens and a new earth.

DISCUSSION QUESTIONS

1. Prior to reading this chapter, what was your understanding of the Old Testament teaching on the Promised Land?
2. Reread Genesis 22:17; 26:3. How do these two verses hint toward a future land possession that will be much more expansive than any earthly territory that Old Testament Israel owned?
3. What is the main purpose of the land, according to the Old Testament? Share some example passages aloud with your group that reinforce this teaching.
4. Read Genesis 15:12-16. What are some of its key insights for understanding the book of Joshua?
5. Why is it important that Christ fulfills the Old Testament hope of land before that inheritance expands to the entire world (e.g., Mt 5:5; Rom 4:13), a new heavens and a new earth (2 Pet 3:13; Rev 21:1-5)?
6. Share something you learned in this chapter that you found particularly insightful and encouraging.

JUDGES

DELIVERING THE REDEEMED

"THE SPOT WAS CANCEROUS but nothing to worry about. It was cut out and won't spread." When I received this text message from my mom, I didn't feel reassured. This was the first I had heard about a spot, and I didn't know who was involved. Through back-and-forth, I learned that my stepdad had noticed an odd-looking spot on his skin. He had visited the doctor right away, and the cancer was entirely removed. Since it was caught early and completely cut out, it would not spread to infect his entire body. Most of us know that even the smallest spot of cancer on the surface of the skin is cause for massive concern *if it is left untreated.*

In the book of Judges, sinful practices among God's people spread like cancer, because unlike the cancerous spot on my stepdad, these practices were left to linger. Throughout the book, the sin of God's people brings on his judgment in the form of enemy oppression, and each time, God raises up a judge to deliver his redeemed.

ESSENTIAL CONTROL OF CANAAN

The book of Judges begins with a summary of Israel's battle victories after the death of Joshua (Judg 1:1-26). This seems promising at first, but just like the book of Joshua, this section also includes whispers of trouble. Although Israel had gained essential control of the Promised

Land in the book of Joshua, and although those conquests continued at the beginning of Judges, there were still many enemies left in the land, and these peoples could easily form pockets of resistance.

Who were these enemies? David J. H. Beldman explains: "The term 'Canaanites' refers to a broad group of people who inhabited Canaan before Israel's conquest. This broad designation consisted of a diversity of ethnicities and nationalities. For example, Judges mentions the Perizzites, Jebusites, Amorites, Philistines, Sidonians, Hivites, and Hittites—all people groups considered Canaanites."[1]

Since many of us live in politically unified countries, we may wrongly assume that the land of Canaan was a politically unified nation. It was not. At this time in history, Canaan was a land filled with city-states, and those city-states were governed by their own kings. Also at this time, Israel was in the process of "maturing from an association of twelve tribes into a fully formed nation."[2]

The key turning point comes in the next chapter, when "all that generation also were gathered to their fathers. And there arose another generation after them who did not know the Lord or the work that he had done for Israel" (Judg 2:10). Although Joshua's generation exhibited many successes and victories, this verse reveals that they also failed to teach their children about YHWH's redemption of Israel as his special people and about YHWH's word, which was to govern them (see Deut 6:4-9). So Israel's covenant disobedience was the root reason they failed to drive out the idolatrous inhabitants of the Promised Land (e.g., Judg 2:2).

A LAND FILLED WITH IDOLS

Beginning in Judges 2, the tone of the book shifts from an account of mostly victories with whispers of trouble (see Judg 1:1-26) to shouts

---

[1]David J. H. Beldman, *Deserting the King: The Book of Judges*, Transformative Word (Lexham, 2017), 62.

[2]Beldman, *Deserting the King*, 2.

of trouble in the form of a long list of peoples Israel had failed to conquer (see Judg 1:27-36). As a result, the angel of YHWH explicitly states, "I will not drive them out before you, but they shall become thorns in your sides, and their gods shall be a snare to you" (Judg 2:3). Just as the fall into sin brought the curse of thorns and thistles for humanity, these nations would be thorns to Israel, and their gods would be snares.[3]

As we noticed in our study of the land theme in Joshua, it was the idolatry of Canaan's inhabitants that provoked YHWH's wrath against them. In contrast to this, God's people were called to be absolutely unique and utterly distinct from the nations as they were governed by YHWH's instruction.[4] When they pursued this radical commitment to YHWH, all the families of the earth would be blessed through them (see Gen 12:3). We already witnessed an initial fulfillment of this when Rahab and her family were incorporated into God's people.

Beldman explains the pagan worldview Israel encountered in Canaan:

> In the ancient Near East, it was customary to worship local deities; these deities were understood to control significant aspects of life like human fertility, crop production, and weather. Those who moved to a new place were expected to identify the deities of that place and worship them so as to ensure prosperity. This was so common in the cultures surrounding Israel that the Israelites likely faced extreme pressure to engage in the worship of the Canaanite gods.[5]

This pressure would have been especially tempting for God's people because their world revolved around the need for crops and children. In the West today, drought in farming communities is very difficult, but

---

[3]I first noticed the link between Judg 2:3 and Gen 3:18 in James M. Hamilton Jr., *God's Glory in Salvation Through Judgment: A Biblical Theology* (Crossway, 2010), 154.

[4]This instruction is summarized in the Ten Words (or Commandments) of Ex 20, but God's people were to be shaped by all of Genesis, Exodus, Leviticus, Numbers, and Deuteronomy.

[5]Beldman, *Deserting the King*, 67.

crop insurance and grocery stores help to stave off complete devastation. In the agricultural world of Bible times, however, drought meant that whole communities would starve. In the West today, it is a great trial when a husband and wife are not able to have children of their own. But in the world of the Bible, kids were a couple's retirement plan, as land would be left for the next generation to farm, and the next generation cared for their parents as they aged.

The shift in Israel's devotion felt subtle at first because they continued to worship YHWH even as they also adopted the gods of their neighbors. Beldman explains once again:

> The problem was not an outright rejection of Yahweh but a synthesis whereby the commitment to Yahweh was filtered through the pagan religion and culture. This helps explain why Jephthah assumed that the promise of human sacrifice would secure Yahweh's favor (Judg 11:30-31) or why Micah thought that an idolatrous shrine with a Levite priest would secure Yahweh's blessing (Judg 17:13).[6]

Even though the shift may have *felt* subtle to Israel, YHWH clearly demands 100 percent of his people's devotion (e.g., Ex 20:3-5).

A DOWNWARD SPIRAL

At the beginning of Judges, the gods of the nations are identified as snares for God's people. The book continues in a downward spiral until Israel is thoroughly *Canaanized*. Instead of being a blessing to all the families of the earth through their faithful covenant relationship with YHWH, they compromise their distinctiveness and become as bad as or worse than their Canaanite neighbors. For this reason, Paul R. House is correct that "the overall impression is one of self-inflicted chaos suffered by a people who forget who they are and how they got to Canaan."[7]

---

[6]Beldman, *Deserting the King*, 86.

[7]Paul R. House, *Old Testament Theology* (InterVarsity Press, 1998), 214.

As Judges 2 continues, there is a summary of the cycle that is repeated six full times in the book. First, we learn that Israel commits nationwide treason against YHWH:

> And the people of Israel did what was evil in the sight of the LORD and served the Baals. And they abandoned the LORD, the God of their fathers, who had brought them out of the land of Egypt. They went after other gods, from among the gods of the peoples who were around them, and bowed down to them. And they provoked the LORD to anger. They abandoned the LORD and served the Baals and the Ashtaroth. So the anger of the LORD was kindled against Israel, and he gave them over to plunderers, who plundered them. And he sold them into the hand of their surrounding enemies, so that they could no longer withstand their enemies. Whenever they marched out, the hand of the LORD was against them for harm, as the LORD had warned, and as the LORD had sworn to them. And they were in terrible distress. (Judg 2:11-15)

Next, we witness YHWH's gracious response to this dire situation: He raises up warrior-deliverers, whom the book calls judges:

> Then the LORD raised up judges, who saved them out of the hand of those who plundered them. Yet they did not listen to their judges, for they whored after other gods and bowed down to them. They soon turned aside from the way in which their fathers had walked, who had obeyed the commandments of the LORD, and they did not do so. Whenever the LORD raised up judges for them, the LORD was with the judge, and he saved them from the hand of their enemies all the days of the judge. For the LORD was moved to pity by their groaning because of those who afflicted and oppressed them. But whenever the judge died, they turned back and were more corrupt than their fathers, going after other gods, serving them and bowing down to them. They did not drop any of their practices or their stubborn ways. So the anger of the LORD was kindled against Israel, and he said, "Because this people have transgressed my covenant that I commanded their fathers

> and have not obeyed my voice, I will no longer drive out before them any of the nations that Joshua left when he died, in order to test Israel by them, whether they will take care to walk in the way of the LORD as their fathers did, or not." So the LORD left those nations, not driving them out quickly, and he did not give them into the hand of Joshua. (Judg 2:16-23)

Peter Gentry summarizes the cycle in four points: "(1) the people break the covenant and sin against Yahweh; (2) Yahweh disciplines them by allowing foreign nations to oppress and harass Israel; (3) the people are called to repentance and cry out for help; and (4) Yahweh raises up a hero or deliverer, called a judge, who rescues the people from their enemies and rules them for a time."[8] This structure helps us understand the rest of the book.

THE STORY OF JUDGES

After the book's introduction in Judges 1:1–3:6, the body of Judges unfolds in six cycles of sin, discipline, cry for help, and deliverer-judge (Judg 3:7–16:31). Interspersed are summary notes about other judges. This is followed by the book's conclusion, in Judges 17:1–21:25. One way of getting a bird's-eye view of the book is to summarize its unfolding story in table form:

Table 2.1. The unfolding story of Judges

Cycle	Oppressor	Oppression	Deliverer	Result	Passage
1	Cushan-Rishathaim king of Mesopotamia	8 years	Othniel, son of Kenaz, Caleb's younger brother	rest for 40 years	Judg 3:7–11
2	Eglon king of Moab, with the Ammonites and the Amalekites	18 years	Ehud, son of Gera, the Benjaminite	rest for 80 years	Judg 3:12–30
—	Philistines	—	Shamgar, son of Anath	—	Judg 3:31

[8]Peter J. Gentry and Stephen J. Wellum, *Kingdom Through Covenant: A Biblical-Theological Understanding of the Covenants*, 2nd ed. (Crossway, 2018), 444.

Cycle	Oppressor	Oppression	Deliverer	Result	Passage
3	Jabin king of Canaan, who reigned in Hazor	20 years	Deborah the prophetess, wife of Lappidoth (along with Barak son of Abinoam from Kedesh-Naphtali)	rest for 40 years	Judg 4:1–5:31
4	Midian	7 years	Gideon, son of Joash the Abiezrite, from Ophrah	rest for 40 years	Judg 6:1–8:35
—	—	—	Tola, son of Puah, son of Dodo, a man of Issachar, from Ephraim	judged Israel for 23 years	Judg 10:1–2
—	—	—	Jair the Gileadite	judged Israel for 22 years	Judg 10:3–5
5	Philistines and Ammonites	18 years	Jephthah the Gileadite, the son of Gilead and a prostitute mother	judged Israel for 6 years	Judg 10:6–12:7
—	—	—	Ibzan of Bethlehem	judged Israel for 7 years	Judg 12:8–10
—	—	—	Elon the Zebulunite	judged Israel for 10 years	Judg 12:11–12
—	—	—	Abdon, son of Hillel the Pirathonite	judged Israel for 8 years	Judg 12:13–15
6	Philistines	40 years	Samson, son of Manoah, from Zorah, of the tribe of the Danites	judged Israel for 20 years	Judg 13:1–16:31
—	civil war	—	—	—	Judg 17:1–21:25

As we see from table 2.1, the story of Judges unfolds in six cycles, highlighted by the story of six major judges: Othniel, Ehud, Deborah, Gideon, Jephthah, and Samson. In between are accounts of minor judges, who are called minor only because their stories are summarized in a verse or two. In each cycle, a different enemy is also encountered. This is because the geography of Judges is scattered throughout the land YHWH promised to his people. For example, Mesopotamia is in the extreme north, Midian in the extreme south, Philistia in the west, and Moab in the east.

This geographical movement provides hints that help us understand the book more deeply. Although Judges presents the story of each judge in light of YHWH's relationship with all of Israel, the judges were regional heroes who fought regional enemies. Since the Promised Land was inhabited by numerous people groups, this makes sense. But Judges is more than a story of a series of distinct enemies; once again Israel itself was in the process of maturing from an association of twelve tribes into a fully formed nation.[9] Sandra L. Richter explains that during this period, the twelve tribes of Israel "lived very independent lives. The only activities that they regularly shared were their joint defense of the Promised Land and their united worship of Yahweh at the tabernacle (which was located primarily at Shiloh). . . . There was no centralized government, no taxation, no joint building projects and no standing army."[10] This means that in the book of Judges, individual tribes in Israel battled against distinct people groups—throughout the Promised Land.

Although Israel was not yet politically unified around a single king, Judges still presents them as a nation. For example, the first cycle reveals that "*the people of Israel* cried out to the LORD," and in response, "the LORD raised up a deliverer *for the people of Israel*, who saved them, Othniel the son of Kenaz, Caleb's younger brother" (Judg 3:9, emphasis added). If the king of Mesopotamia oppressed the tribe of Judah *in the south*, and if YHWH responded to his people's cries by

---

[9]See Beldman, *Deserting the King*, 2.

[10]Sandra L. Richter, *The Epic of Eden: A Christian Entry into the Old Testament* (IVP Academic, 2008), 191.

raising up Othniel of Judah as a deliverer, why does the wording of Judges make it sound as though the oppression and deliverance was *national*? While Israel was still in the process of maturing into a fully formed nation, in YHWH's eyes they *were* a singular people group. He had delivered *Israel* from Egypt, and he was about to bring political unity to *Israel*—through a king in the book of Samuel. As Judges tells the story of the time between the exodus from Egypt and the monarchy, it makes clear that YHWH viewed his people as one.

The geographical movement in the book also reveals something about the rebellion and unbelief among God's people: It was total. It is not as though one tribe in Israel rebelled against YHWH and so was oppressed by one enemy. The entire nation was corrupt, whether in the north, south, east, west, or any place in between.

It is helpful to make another observation about the way the story of Judges is told: It recounts accurate historical information, but it reads very differently from news sources we encounter today. Instead of simply telling us the bare *facts* of what happened, Judges focuses on the spiritual causes and effects behind the events it reports. Andreas Köstenberger and Gregory Goswell explain:

> God is actively exercising his role as King over his people. God is involved in both the punishment and the deliverance of Israel. He "sold" them into the hands of Cushan-rishathaim, Jabin, the Philistines, and the Ammonites (Judg. 3:8; 4:2; 10:7); he "gave them into the hand" of the Midianites and the Philistines (6:1, 13; 13:1); and he "strengthened" Eglon, king of Moab, against Israel (3:12). At the same time, YHWH's involvement in saving Israel is made plain (e.g., Samson's birth is a miracle [13:2-3]). He gives Israel's enemies into their hands (Judg. 3:10, 28; 4:7, 14-15; 7:2, 7, 9, 14-15; 8:3, 7; 11:9, 30, 32; 12:3), and the Spirit of the Lord falls on a judge before he goes into battle (3:10; 6:34; 11:29; 13:25; 14:6, 19; 15:14).[11]

[11]Andreas J. Köstenberger and Gregory Goswell, *Biblical Theology: A Canonical, Thematic, and Ethical Approach* (Crossway, 2023), 173.

Judges tells the story of Israel *theologically*, with God at the center. As we read this book, we learn to view our own lives through the lens of God's involvement in our world. In fact, God is the main character in this book, and indeed the entire Bible.

Even more than the geographical movement in the book, Judges also presents its cycles as a downward spiral. The book reports six full cycles of sin, oppression, repentance, and deliverance by a judge. As these progress, we discover a general movement from shorter to longer oppression at the hands of enemy nations—from eight years before YHWH raised up Othniel (Judg 3:7-11) to forty years before he raised up Samson (Judg 13:1–16:31). The opposite is true for the result of the judge's deliverance: The first four cycles result in YHWH giving the land rest for at least forty years after the death of the judge. But in the last two cycles, there is no report of rest, and Israel is safe only until Jephthah and Samson die. As the story unfolds, oppression increases and rest decreases to nothing. The downward spiral reaches its lowest point in the book's conclusion (Judg 17:1–21:25), when civil war and horrible sin mean that Israel's greatest enemy is itself.

FLAWED HEROES

Who were these judges? The Hebrew root behind the term "to judge" can refer to someone who either "decides between" or who "rules," depending on the context.[12] G. F. Moore adds that in the context of the book as a whole, the word means "'defend,' 'deliver,' 'avenge,' and 'punish' as well as to 'rule' or 'govern.'"[13] Since the figures in the book of Judges were military heroes, the NIV 2011 and NET Bible insightfully translate this word "to lead" (see Judg 3:10; 4:4; 10:2-3; 12:9, 11, 13;

[12]See Bruce K. Waltke and Charles Yu, *An Old Testament Theology: An Exegetical, Canonical, and Thematic Approach* (Zondervan, 2007), 588.

[13]House, *Old Testament Theology*, 217, citing George Foot Moore, *A Critical and Exegetical Commentary on Judges*, International Critical Commentary (Scribner's, 1895), xi.

15:20; 16:31; 1 Sam 4:18; 7:15).[14] Whenever we encounter the term "to judge" in other English translations, we need to remind ourselves that the Hebrew word carries the meaning "to lead" in the book of Judges. These were not Supreme Court justices; they were military heroes.

On the one hand, these leader-judges accomplished superhuman military defeats. For example, Samson struck down one thousand Philistines in hand-to-hand combat, with the jawbone of a donkey as his only weapon (Judg 15:15-16). As we have seen, these victories were ultimately from YHWH. In fact, Samson's defeat of the Philistines came because "the Spirit of the LORD rushed upon him" (Judg 15:14).

On the other hand, these leader-judges were extremely flawed and sinful. Although every one of the Bible's human heroes (other than Jesus) has feet of clay, the leader-judges were especially brutal. For example, as Jephthah is advancing on the Ammonites, he vows, "If you will give the Ammonites into my hand, then whatever comes out from the doors of my house to meet me when I return in peace from the Ammonites shall be the LORD's, and I will offer it up for a burnt offering" (Judg 11:30-31). It is true that at this time and place in history, "the narrower side rooms [on the ground floor of houses] functioned as stables and shelters for livestock."[15] However, when Jephthah approaches his house after a long and dangerous trip, who is more likely to come out first: a family member or an animal? Whatever the odds, he is willing to take the risk.

The story unfolds in the worst possible way, as the first to emerge from Jephthah's house is his virgin daughter. As Bruce Waltke puts it, this "rash vow comes tantalizingly close to the Ammonite practice of child sacrifice."[16] Lest we think it noble that Jephthah and his daughter go through with the vow, recall that "the sixth of the

[14]I was pointed to this list of passages in Waltke and Yu, *Old Testament Theology*, 588. See also Köstenberger and Goswell, *Biblical Theology*, 168.

[15]Philip J. King and Lawrence E. Stager, *Life in Biblical Israel* (Westminster John Knox, 2001), 34; cf. 29; as cited in Waltke and Yu, *Old Testament Theology*, 606.

[16]Waltke and Yu, *Old Testament Theology*, 606.

Ten Commandments forbids murder, and God does not want a vow that violates his Law and is abhorrent to him. Moreover the Law (Lev. 18:21; 20:2; Deut. 12:31) and the Prophets (Jer. 19:5; Ezek. 20:30-31; 23:37, 39) forbid child sacrifice."[17] This is just one of many examples of horrendous sins in the leader-judges. They were flawed heroes who were not fully formed by YHWH's instructions in living as his people (see Ex 20–24).

A TRAGIC ENDING

The downward spiral in Judges climaxes in the book's conclusion, where a man named Micah steals his mother's silver, breaking the fifth and eighth commandments (see Ex 20:12, 15).[18] After he confesses his crime, his mother dedicates it to YHWH and commissions her son to have some of it made into an idol, breaking the first three commandments (see Ex 20:3-7). Micah then puts the idol in his house, along with an ephod and some other idols, where he also employs a Levite as his priest. In the next chapter, the tribe of Dan steals those gods, along with the Levite, once again breaking the eighth commandment (Judg 18). After military victory, the Danites gain an inheritance, and we learn that "the people of Dan set up the carved image for themselves, and Jonathan the son of Gershom, son of Moses, and his sons were priests to the tribe of the Danites until the day of the captivity of the land. So they set up Micah's carved image that he made, as long as the house of God was at Shiloh" (Judg 18:30-31). In this scene, the entire tribe is committing idolatry, and a *grandson of Moses* and his sons are their priests. Notice that it took only three generations for Israel's sin to spiral this low.[19]

---

[17]Waltke and Yu, *Old Testament Theology*, 607.

[18]I first got the idea for tracking broken commandments at the end of Judges from J. Barton Payne, *The Theology of the Older Testament* (Zondervan, 1962), 335-36, as cited in House, *Old Testament Theology*, 223.

[19]Another possibility is that "son of" refers to "descendant of," meaning that there could have been gaps in the genealogy.

Next comes the strange story of a Levite and his concubine, filled with sexual sin, murder, and covetousness, breaking the sixth, seventh, and tenth commandments (see Ex 20:13-14; 17). In this scene, the Levite and his concubine choose not to go to the city of Jebus, which at the time was not yet inhabited by Israelites. Instead, they go to Gibeah (Judg 19:12). In that Israelite stronghold, the Levite's concubine becomes the victim of a grotesque sexual assault that results in her death. As Dempster puts it, this story "thunderously echoes the depravity of Sodom (Gen. 19:4-9; Judg. 19:22-25). Israel has become Sodom!"[20] When the Levite finds the concubine dead in the morning, he takes her body and sets out. Then, "when he entered his house, he took a knife, and taking hold of his concubine he divided her, limb by limb, into twelve pieces, and sent her throughout all the territory of Israel" (Judg 19:29). This grisly action shouts a clear message: All of Israel has become unclean and so is not fit to worship YHWH.

In the last two chapters of Judges, the downward spiral continues. As Gentry and Dempster put it, "'A holy war must be conducted on the people of God' (Judg. 20–21)."[21] In the civil war that follows, the Israelite tribe of Benjamin is decimated to near-extinction, with only a few remaining survivors (Judg 20:47). The book of Judges certainly helps us to stand in horror of sin and its horrible consequences.

AN OMINOUS REFRAIN

No wonder the conclusion of Judges is bookended by an ominous refrain: "In those days there was no king in Israel. Everyone did what was right in his own eyes" (Judg 17:6, cf. Judg 21:25; also Judg 18:1; 19:1). On the one hand, the downward spiral in Judges climaxes to a point at which the entire land is unclean (Judg 19:29) and at which the Israelites themselves are shocked by the level of their own depravity

[20]Stephen G. Dempster, *Dominion and Dynasty: A Theology of the Hebrew Bible*, New Studies in Biblical Theology 15 (InterVarsity Press, 2003), 131.

[21]Dempster, *Dominion and Dynasty*, 131. Dempster credits Peter Gentry with the exact wording of "holy war" in this quotation.

(Judg 19:30). Combined with our observations about the repeated breaking of the Ten Commandments, it is clear that YHWH is not their king, and so everyone does what is right in their own eyes.

On the other hand, this ominous refrain leads us to look for a solution, and that solution comes in the next book of the Old Testament: Samuel. In fact, other judges are mentioned in 1 Samuel: Eli (1 Sam 4:18), Samuel (1 Sam 7:6-17), and Samuel's sons, Joel and Abijah (1 Sam 8:1-2). But in this next book, the time of the judges is eclipsed with the institution of kingship, especially in David. YHWH's chosen king will be tasked with restraining "the evil of the people by enforcing the law of Yahweh, just as Deuteronomy 17:18-20 stipulates."[22] As we will see in chapter three, Samuel is tasked with identifying YHWH's choice of leader who will unite the nation and lead them in righteousness.

LOOKING FORWARD TO CHRIST: A BETTER DELIVERER THAN SAMSON

Near the end of his letter, the author of Hebrews wrote a forty-verse section that has been aptly called the great hall of faith. This chapter combs through the Old Testament for examples of faith, which the author defines as "the assurance of things hoped for, the conviction of things not seen" (Heb 11:1). From creation to Abel, Enoch, Noah, Abraham, Sarah, Isaac, Jacob, Joseph, Moses, the Israelites at the Red Sea, the warriors surrounding Jericho, and Rahab, this is quite a list of faith-filled Old Testament superstars. No wonder the author moves from these examples of faith to an exhortation to follow their lead:

> Therefore, since we are surrounded by so great a cloud of witnesses, let us also lay aside every weight, and sin which clings so closely, and let us run with endurance the race that is set before us, looking to Jesus, the founder and perfecter of our faith, who for the joy that was set

[22]Hamilton, *God's Glory in Salvation Through Judgment*, 157.

> before him endured the cross, despising the shame, and is seated at the right hand of the throne of God. (Heb 12:1-2)

Just as the Israelites followed the cloud of YHWH's presence by day, Christians should follow a *cloud of witnesses* in the examples of Old Testament saints, says the author of Hebrews.

Near the end of Hebrews 11, the author summarizes some additional faith-filled figures from the Old Testament: "And what more shall I say? For time would fail me to tell of Gideon, Barak, Samson, Jephthah, of David and Samuel and the prophets" (Heb 11:32). A key lesson from this verse is simple: Christians should dig deeply into the books of Old Testament history, looking for examples of faith.

Although Hebrews 11:32 is encouraging on the surface, when we actually go back and read the Old Testament accounts of these figures, we will likely be appalled. Why? Because the book of Judges chronicles the moral failures of Gideon, Barak, Samson, and Jephthah. How can they also be named in Hebrews 11:32 as models of faith whom Christians should follow?

To help answer this question, we can consider a lesson from my family's home movies. When my kids were young, my wife and I stood at the sidelines of countless soccer and baseball fields, and in freezing arenas for hockey games, always with a video recorder in hand. During those games, we watched as our kids were guilty of turnovers that resulted in goals for the opposing team, strikeouts with the bases loaded, and shots that missed an open net. After the game, though, those were not the things we talked about as a family. Instead, we celebrated the *successes* of our kids. They may have only touched the soccer ball *one time*, but we watched *that* video clip with delight (and deleted the end, where the opposing team intercepted the pass and went on to score). They may have only made contact with one baseball, and it may have resulted in a double play, but as we watched the home movie we encouraged their emerging hand-eye coordination. The opposing goalie may have stopped their shot on net, but we delighted in footage of their skating stride and quick shot.

Hebrews 11 teaches us that *God is like a proud parent at his child's sporting event.* As God looks at our Christian life, he loves to celebrate every single success of faith, even though there is still a long way for us to go in this life of faith. Why? Because in every single triumph of faith, God sees his Son in us. Also, in every single triumph of faith, God sees *growth.* This is not to make light of the gravity of our sin or the sins of Gideon, Barak, Samson, and Jephthah: Sin always leaves destruction in its wake. But as we see these judges' names in Hebrews 11:32, we learn a lesson in *grace.*

Before I close, there is one more amazing truth from the life of the judges. Not only do their lives exhibit many important examples of faith that Christians today should follow, but they also point us to one to come who is a much *better* deliverer. We have seen some of the various judges' successes and failures. They were extraordinary deliverers for YHWH's people, but their sins were also great. In many ways their lives point us to Jesus, who accomplished the ultimate deliverance for all who would turn from their sins and trust in him. On the cross, Jesus accomplished the deliverance of a multitude of people from eternal death to eternal life. In powerful *contrast* to the judges, however, *Jesus never sinned*: "We do not have a high priest who is unable to sympathize with our weaknesses, but one who in every respect has been tempted as we are, yet without sin" (Heb 4:15). Jesus was tempted in every way Gideon, Barak, Samson, and Jephthah were tempted, and he was tempted in every way that we are tempted. *Yet he was (and is) without sin.*

This means that Jesus was able to be the ultimate sacrifice. Because of his absolute moral purity, he could be offered in our place and accomplish the ultimate deliverance from the ultimate enemy, *for us.* How are we to respond to this awesome gospel truth? With confidence: "Let us then with confidence draw near to the throne of grace, that we may receive mercy and find grace to help in time of need" (Heb 4:16). The one who died for our sins is calling us.

DISCUSSION QUESTIONS

1. Read Judges 2:10 with your group. What did this failure result in for God's people? How does this negative example encourage a much better way for parents today? Give specific examples.
2. What were some factors that led to idolatry as a particular temptation for Israel? What are some idols that we may be tempted to worship today? Hint: Read Ephesians 5:5 and Colossians 3:5 and share some concrete expressions of this sin that are alive and well in our own lives.
3. David J. H. Beldman shows that Israel didn't think they were rejecting YHWH when they *added* the worship of other gods to their worship of YHWH. What are some ways Christians may be tempted to make similar compromises in our day?
4. How does the book of Judges report its events differently from, say, Fox News or CNN? What lessons does this teach?
5. What lessons can be drawn from the grotesque sexual assault and grisly conclusion to the story of the Levite and his concubine (see Judg 19:29-30)?
6. Why does the author of Hebrews include names such as Gideon, Barak, Samson, and Jephthah in the great hall of faith (Heb 11:32)?

KINGS

LEADING AND REPRESENTING THE REDEEMED

On September 8, 2022, many Western countries went into mourning. After a seventy-year reign—the longest in British history—Queen Elizabeth II had died at the age of ninety-six. Eleven days of ceremonies followed, and these were capped off by a state funeral. She was the only monarch most British citizens had ever known.

For many of us in the Western world, Britain has the only monarchy we have ever been familiar with. This means that many of us transfer what we know about the British monarchy to our Bible reading about kings. While there may be some overlap, there are also some differences. For example, the king's power in the ancient Near East was not balanced by another leader who was elected into office—such as the prime minister in Britain. These and other distinctions are important as we soak in the Bible's teaching so we can apply its rich theology to our lives. This chapter will focus on the rise of kings in Israel, with Saul and David. In chapter five, we'll look closer at the story of the Old Testament kings after David.

THE KING AS REPRESENTATIVE HEAD

One important way Old Testament kings differed from British monarchs is in the biblical concept of the king as the representative head of his people. While Western readers most often operate with an individualistic worldview, the Old Testament presents a corporate solidarity between the king and his people.[1] Walter Kaiser explains that in this mindset, "the whole group is able to function as a single individual through one of its members."[2] Although the king and his subjects were each individually accountable before YHWH, the king's life also represented his people before YHWH. As Peter Gentry puts it, only Israel's king could say, "I am Israel" and also be distinguished from Israel.[3]

This insight helps us understand some Old Testament passages that may have previously confused us. For example, why would YHWH put seventy thousand men in Israel to death because of King David's sinful actions (see 2 Sam 24:15)? With the king as their representative head, the entire community was guilty because they had sinned in the actions of their king.

In fact, this concept may not be as unfamiliar to us Western Christians as we first thought, because it also explains the gospel. The Bible teaches that all humanity is under one of two representative heads: Adam or Jesus (see Rom 5:12-21). As the apostle Paul puts it, "As one trespass [by Adam] led to condemnation for all [people], so one act of righteousness [by Christ] leads to justification and life for all [people]" (Rom 5:18). According to Paul, all people are born "in Adam" and are thus guilty before God. However, all who turn from their sin and trust Christ's work for them are "in Christ" and so justified before God (e.g., Rom 3:24; 6:23; 8:1-2). The only difference is that unlike Old Testament kings—such as David, whose sin as representative head led to punishment for his people—our representative head is sinless

---

[1]I cover this same concept in a similar though complementary manner in Ian J. Vaillancourt, *Treasuring the Psalms: How to Read the Songs That Shape the Soul of the Church* (IVP Academic, 2023), 79-94.

[2]Walter C. Kaiser Jr., *The Christian and the Old Testament* (William Carey Library, 2012), 175.

[3]See Peter J. Gentry and Stephen J. Wellum, *Kingdom Through Covenant: A Biblical-Theological Understanding of the Covenants,* 2nd ed. (Crossway, 2018), 495.

(Heb 4:15). This means that under the new covenant, Christians will *never* be found guilty, because we are in Christ. We will only ever be counted righteous in him. Praise YHWH!

THE ANTICIPATED, IDEAL KING

"Dad, come out and help us!" My kids had been rolling a snowball outside, but very quickly it had become too big and heavy for them—they needed help. I arrived on the scene and continued to roll it some more—with two little helpers pushing on my back. Pretty soon, though, a snowball that began its life the size of a child's hand was too heavy for an adult (and his two helpers) to budge.

As we approach the Bible's teaching on the coming Messiah, we find that it begins small, with the promise of a serpent-crushing Savior (Gen 3:15). But as the Old Testament progresses, this teaching snowballs as more details are added. Very quickly after this initial promise, we learn that the coming savior will be a king, and as the story unfolds, we learn a great deal more about what kind of king he will be.

The first hints are found in promises that kings will come from the lineage of Abraham and his grandson Jacob (Gen 17:6, 16; 35:11). This becomes more specific, however, as the elderly Jacob blesses his sons and points out one as most prominent: "The scepter shall not depart from Judah, nor the ruler's staff from between his feet, until tribute comes to him; and to him shall be the obedience of the peoples" (Gen 49:10). In this verse, we learn that Judah's lineage will carry the scepter/ruler's staff—kings will come from him. And this will be perpetual—the scepter/ruler's staff will not depart from him. According to the first book of the Old Testament, YHWH will accomplish salvation for his people through perpetual kingship in the lineage of Abraham, Jacob, and Judah.

After another promise of a coming king who will deliver God's people (Num 24:17), we encounter specific teaching about the ideal king. When they settle into the Promised Land, YHWH permits his people to set a king over them,

> whom the LORD your God will choose. One from among your brothers you shall set as king over you. You may not put a foreigner over you, who is not your brother. Only he must not acquire many horses for himself or cause the people to return to Egypt in order to acquire many horses, since the LORD has said to you, "You shall never return that way again." And he shall not acquire many wives for himself, lest his heart turn away, nor shall he acquire for himself excessive silver and gold.
>
> And when he sits on the throne of his kingdom, he shall write for himself in a book a copy of this law, approved by the Levitical priests. And it shall be with him, and he shall read in it all the days of his life, that he may learn to fear the LORD his God by keeping all the words of this law and these statutes, and doing them, that his heart may not be lifted up above his brothers, and that he may not turn aside from the commandment, either to the right hand or to the left, so that he may continue long in his kingdom, he and his children, in Israel. (Deut 17:15-20)

This means that Israel is not to model its kingship after the wicked nations around them. They are to appoint a king whom YHWH their God will choose. He is required to be an Israelite. Instead of trusting in horses or riches (i.e., defense spending and economic growth), he will lead the people in trusting YHWH. Unlike the rulers in the polygamous cultures around them, he is not to acquire many wives. And he needs to be absolutely steeped in the Word of God, writing out his own personal copy, getting it checked for accuracy by a priest, and reading from it every day of his life. Israel's king needs to be humble, immersed in God's Word, and righteous before God. As we remember that the king represented the people before YHWH, we can see why this ideal blueprint in Deuteronomy 17:14-20 is so essential.

In this context, 1 Samuel begins with a miraculous birth to an elderly couple. Although baby Samuel will grow to be a priest (1 Sam 2:35), prophet (1 Sam 3:19-21), and judge (1 Sam 7:15), at his birth his mother sings a song of praise—the Magnificat of the Old Testament—that concludes with a prophecy that YHWH will raise up a *king*: "The Lord will judge the ends of the earth; he will give strength to his king and exalt the horn of his anointed" (1 Sam 2:10).[4]

All of this means that Israel's king was not an accident of history. Long before Saul, David, Solomon, or any of the kings who followed, YHWH revealed that a king would be an integral part of his plan to bring ultimate salvation to his people. This ruler sounds wonderful, doesn't he? YHWH will be with him. He will be strong and victorious. He will be a model of faithfulness to YHWH in every way. But as we will see, every king in the Old Testament falls short of the portrait of this anticipated, ideal king.

THE ACTUAL, IMPERFECT KING

Saul's rise, rejection, and successor. Between the promise of an ideal king and the birth of the Lord Jesus as the perfect, ultimate king (Mt 2:2), we see the rise of kingship in Israel in the books of Samuel and Kings. Many of these kings exhibit glimmers of greatness, but when we survey their lives through the lens of the ideal king the Bible had promised, we quickly find that each one falls woefully short. We begin with the Bible's introduction of Israel's first king, Saul: "There was a man of Benjamin whose name was Kish . . . a Benjaminite, a man of wealth. And he had a son whose name was Saul, a handsome young man. There was not a man among the people of Israel more handsome than he. From his shoulders upward he was taller than any of the people" (1 Sam 9:1-2). What is wrong with this description? Instead of being from Judah (Gen 49:10), Saul is from the tribe of Benjamin. Instead of being chosen for his character (Deut 17:14-20),

---

[4]See Stephen G. Dempster, *The Return of the Kingdom: A Biblical Theology of God's Reign* (IVP Academic, 2024), 115. The song of Mary in Lk 1:46-55 has been called the Magnificat, its first word in Latin. *Magnificat* means "it praises" (referring to Mary's heart).

Saul is chosen because of his stature: He is tall and handsome. Choosing him is the opposite of trusting in YHWH for victory. While the ideal king will be steeped in YHWH's Word, there is no mention of God's Word in this description of Saul. As careful readers of the Old Testament, we are not expecting things to go well.

As the story unfolds, we discover that Saul lacks courage from the beginning. For instance, after he is chosen as king, he hides from the people (1 Sam 10:22). Although he leads Israel's armies to victory (e.g., 1 Sam 13:1-4), he also disregards YHWH's word on two important occasions—he acts as a priest when Samuel is late to the scene, and he also fails to carry out YHWH's instructions in victory over the Amalekites (1 Sam 13:8-15; 15:8-9). For these reasons, YHWH reveals that Saul's kingdom will not continue. He has rejected the word of YHWH, so YHWH rejects him (1 Sam 13:14; 15:26).

With Saul still alive, YHWH sends Samuel to the house of Jesse to anoint one of his sons as his chosen king. From the beginning, things look promising: Jesse is from the tribe of *Judah*, and the young, humble David is chosen because YHWH looks on the heart (1 Sam 16:7, 11-13). After his anointing as king, David enters into service for Saul as his personal musician and armor bearer (1 Sam 16:14-23).

Will David emerge as the ideal king YHWH promised? Things continue to look hopeful when the young, small David is victorious over a Philistine giant named Goliath (1 Sam 17). When Saul's jealousy leads to attempted murder, David runs for his life to caves in the wilderness (e.g., 1 Sam 22). Although he has the chance to kill Saul on several occasions, he will not do such a thing to YHWH's (imperfect, rejected) anointed king (e.g., 1 Sam 24; 26). As long as Saul is alive, David—the rightful king—will live in tension.

So far, the Bible's portrait of David has been nothing but positive. As the story progresses, however, we get hints that even David will not live up to YHWH's promise of the ideal king. For example, when he is wronged by a foolish man named Nabal, David responds with a resolve to kill this man and every other male in his household (1 Sam 25:22). It is only through the intervention of Nabal's wife that YHWH spares David from the bloodguilt that would have come from avenging himself (1 Sam 25:32-34). This means that David is clearly capable of murder—something forbidden of all God's people (see Ex 20:13). Although David is already married to Saul's daughter, Michal, he takes two more wives: Nabal's widow, Abigail, and Ahinoam of Jezreel (1 Sam 25:39-43). When Saul gives David's first wife to another man for marriage, the soap opera of his life is complete, with two current wives and one ex-wife. He is certainly not living up to the ideal portrait: "And [the king] shall not acquire many wives for himself, lest his heart turn away" (Deut 17:17).

First Samuel 25 acts like a movie spoiler does today—we are given a hint at how the story will end before it really gets started. David's murderous intent against Nabal, and his polygamy with Abigail and Ahinoam, hint that he will ultimately fall short. Although David will be the greatest human king in the entire Old Testament, even he will not live up to the standards of the coming king, who will be YHWH's means of accomplishing ultimate victory for his people.

YHWH's covenant with David. After the death of Saul, David's reign begins in Hebron and then spreads over all Israel (2 Sam 2:1-7; 5:1-5). At the beginning of his rise to power, however, we discover that David has accumulated *six* wives, and then he steals Michal back from her weeping second husband (2 Sam 3:2-5, 12-16). Later, David takes even more wives and then adds concubines as well (2 Sam 5:13). These sobering failures act as previews to other, greater failures to come.

First, however, we encounter great blessings. In 2 Samuel 6, the ark of the covenant is brought to Jerusalem—this is the first centralized location for Israel and its king. It is also a settled place for YHWH's special presence—the tabernacle no longer needs to move around because YHWH's people are staying put.

Bruce Springsteen sings a catchy song about the way middle-aged people (like me!) love to look back on the glory days of their youth, when life seemed more carefree. If Bruce Springsteen were singing a song about the glory days of the Old Testament story, he would look back wistfully on the scene in 2 Samuel 7.

In 2 Samuel 7:1-14, YHWH makes an incredible promise to David—a scene that later Scripture confirms was a *covenant* between YHWH and David (see 2 Sam 23:5; 2 Chron 21:7; Is 55:3; Jer 33:21; Ps 89:3, 28, 34, 39; 132:12). In the Pentateuch we discover four covenants between YHWH and his people: with creation (Gen 1:26-30; 2:15-25), with Noah (Gen 6:9–9:17), with Abraham (Gen 15:1-21; 17:1-27), and with Moses/Israel (Ex 19–24). After this fifth covenant, between YHWH and David, a sixth will follow—the new covenant promised in the prophets (see Jer 31:31-34; Ezek 36:26-28) and fulfilled by Christ (e.g., Lk 22:20; 1 Cor 11:25).[5]

As I write elsewhere, "While the larger story of the Bible is indeed a story of God's redemption, the six covenants between YHWH and his people are high points in the larger story. They drive the story of redemption forward because they formalize YHWH's commitment, detail his terms, and guarantee a glorious outcome."[6] YHWH's covenant with David builds on his previous commitments:

- to provide life, abundance, and his special presence (creation)
- never again to destroy all life by a flood (Noah)
- to make Abraham into a great people with an abundant land (Abraham)
- to be Israel's God and for Israel to be his people (Moses/Israel)

Now, in his covenant with David, YHWH promises to build him *a house.*

---

[5]For a more in-depth look at covenants in the Old Testament, see Ian J. Vaillancourt, *The Dawning of Redemption: The Story of the Pentateuch and the Hope of the Gospel* (Crossway, 2022), 89-109.
[6]Vaillancourt, *Dawning of Redemption*, 91.

What does YHWH mean? Here is the heart of YHWH's covenant promise to David:

> I will make for you a great name, like the name of the great ones of the earth. And I will appoint a place for my people Israel and will plant them, so that they may dwell in their own place and be disturbed no more. And violent men shall afflict them no more, as formerly, from the time that I appointed judges over my people Israel. And I will give you rest from all your enemies. Moreover, the LORD declares to you that the LORD will make you a house. When your days are fulfilled and you lie down with your fathers, I will raise up your offspring after you, who shall come from your body, and I will establish his kingdom. He shall build a house for my name, and I will establish the throne of his kingdom forever. I will be to him a father, and he shall be to me a son. (2 Sam 7:9-14)

David's name first appears at his anointing as king in 1 Samuel 16:13, but it will be found 1,075 times in the Hebrew Old Testament and another fifty-nine times in the Greek New Testament, for a total of 1,134 occurrences in the Bible. Along with Abraham and Moses, David is among the greatest figures in the Old Testament, and his life ultimately points to the greater Son of David to come, the Lord Jesus. YHWH certainly made him a great name, like the great ones of the earth (see 2 Sam 7:9).

David's life also ushers in a period of settledness and peace for YHWH's people (2 Sam 7:10-11). YHWH will make David a *house*, a line of descendants who will reign (2 Sam 7:11-14). Although the initial son of David, Solomon, will sin greatly, YHWH will not cast him off as he did with Saul—he will discipline him instead (2 Sam 7:14-15). David's throne—with a descendant who will reign over God's people—will be established *forever* (2 Sam 7:16). This was fulfilled after the resurrection and ascension of Jesus, when he took his eternal place at YHWH's right hand on the throne of the cosmos (see Ps 110:1; Heb 1:3; etc.).

David's horrible failures. Though we have encountered many setbacks in the Bible's story of redemption, YHWH's redeemed people have made many advances under David—especially in YHWH's covenant with him. They have settled into their own land, have enjoyed a season of relative peace, and have the promised king reigning over them. What could go wrong?

After YHWH's covenant with him, things quickly deteriorate when David uses his power to have sex with the married Bathsheba (2 Sam 11). When we pay attention to the verbs used in the story, it becomes clear that she doesn't have a choice in the matter—David is the initiator. In 2 Samuel 11:2-4, we learn that David "saw . . . sent . . . inquired . . . sent . . . took . . . lay with" Bathsheba. Then, when his attempt to cover up the unwanted pregnancy fails, he devises a plan to have her husband murdered (2 Sam 11:14-17). After the prophet Nathan exposes his grave sins, David repents, but he also bears consequences, as YHWH declares: "Behold, I will raise up evil against you out of your own house. And I will take your wives before your eyes and give them to your neighbor, and he shall lie with your wives in the sight of this sun" (2 Sam 12:11).

This meant that David's family strife in 2 Samuel 13–18 is not a coincidence—the prophet Nathan directly connects it to YHWH's discipline for David's grave sins. Finally, before the end of his reign, David's sinful heart is shown to trust in the size of his army instead of YHWH (2 Sam 24). For this reason, YHWH puts seventy thousand men of Israel to death—if David wants to trust in soldiers instead of YHWH, his covenant God will put a massive number of those soldiers to death in an instant. As we recall the inseparable link between the king and the people over whom he was covenant head, we remember that far from being unfair (as our individualistic Western minds might conclude), the sin of the king made an entire people *guilty*.

If David's flawed but glorious reign was the glory days for God's Old Testament people, we encounter a few glimmers of hope after his death. For example, Solomon builds the Jerusalem temple as a fixed place where YHWH will dwell (1 Kings 6). Even foreigners, such as the queen of Sheba, are blessed by Solomon's wisdom (1 Kings 10:1-13; cf. Gen 22:18). Under Solomon, Israel's land also expands. However, Solomon's sins outdo those of David. As we continue the story of Israel's kings in a later chapter, we'll notice that their downward spiral into sin ultimately leads God's people into division, decline, and exile.

LOOKING FORWARD TO CHRIST: DAVID, GOLIATH, AND THE GOSPEL

Although David and the other Old Testament kings exhibited great acts of faith, they also displayed great failures. This reminds us once again that the real hero of the Bible is God. Even still, God designed the Bible with patterns that begin in the Old Testament and point to a greater fulfillment in Christ. Although David was a great sinner—guilty of grave sexual sin, murder, and faithlessness—his life as king over God's people points to an even greater, ultimate Son of David to come. One such scene is the story of David and Goliath, found in 1 Samuel 17.[7]

Who doesn't love a story of an underdog-hero who wins an unexpected victory over a giant enemy? Books and movies have grown out of this scene, and the lesson they often draw out is inspiring: Just like David defeated the giant in his life with God's help, so you and I can overcome any giant obstacle in our lives with God's help. However, as we look at the story of David and Goliath in light of the sweep of the Bible's story, we discover gospel application that is much richer than the common facing-your-giants lesson.

---

[7]For another accessible though fuller treatment of the David and Goliath story, see Ian J. Vaillancourt, *David, Goliath, and the Gospel: Living in Light of Our Savior's Victory*, Discovery Series (Our Daily Bread Ministries, 2021).

We have already noticed that the Old Testament anticipates a savior who will crush the serpent's head (Gen 3:15), be a righteous king in the family lineage of Judah (Gen 49:10; Deut 17:14-20), and accomplish great victory for God's people (1 Sam 2:10). A simple observation unlocks the story of David and Goliath: 1 Samuel 16 (where Samuel anoints David as king) comes *before* 1 Samuel 17 (where David defeats Goliath). This means that the young boy named David who conquered the giant enemy was not merely "just like us." He was YHWH's choice as king over his people, Israel. In the context of the Bible's grand story, the victory of David over Goliath signals something wonderful and hopeful: David *may* be the king who will accomplish salvation for YHWH's people. At the very least, he may accomplish great things and point forward to an ultimate Son of David to come.

First Samuel 17 begins with brutal hand-to-hand combat between Israel and the Philistines, who have a giant warrior named Goliath fighting for them. Every morning for forty days and nights, this giant taunts God's people: "Choose a man for yourselves, and let him come down to me. If he is able to fight with me and kill me, then we will be your servants. But if I prevail against him and kill him, then you shall be our servants and serve us" (1 Sam 17:8-9). The people—including Saul, who is the tallest man of Israel—are "dismayed and greatly afraid" (1 Sam 17:11).

David enters the scene as the kid brother sent to bring supplies to his older siblings and then a report of the war back to his dad. But when he hears the taunts of Goliath, he is indignant at the mockery of his God and decides to take up the challenge. After gathering some stones from a stream, he approaches the giant and says,

> You come to me with a sword and with a spear and with a javelin, but I come to you in the name of the LORD of hosts, the God of the armies of Israel, whom you have defied. This day the LORD will deliver you into my hand, and I will strike you down and cut off your head. And I will give the dead bodies of the host of the Philistines this day to the

> birds of the air and to the wild beasts of the earth, that all the earth may know that there is a God in Israel, and that all this assembly may know that the LORD saves not with sword and spear. For the battle is the LORD's, and he will give you into our hand. (1 Sam 17:45-47)

David runs toward the giant enemy, slings a stone, downs him with a perfect shot to the forehead, and then runs up and cuts off his head (see Gen 3:15, where the coming Savior will crush the head of the seed of the serpent).[8] In response, the warriors of Israel chase and rout the defeated Philistine army. The victory has been won *for them*, so they actively participate in the battle. Before David defeated Goliath, the warriors of Israel were fighting *for* victory. After David defeated Goliath, the warriors of Israel were fighting *from* victory.[9]

While we can relate in some ways to David as an underdog who faced this very difficult challenge, we need to remember that *David was also more than "just like us."* As the covenant head over God's people, David points us forward to the ultimate king who will win an even better victory in even greater weakness.

At the beginning and end of his life, Jesus' weakness and vulnerability are linked to his role as the ultimate Son of David, the coming king who will fulfill the Old Testament hope. But as the ultimate Son of David, Jesus is better. He is God the Son, the Second Person of the Trinity. Yet unlike David, Jesus *chooses* to become weak and vulnerable, *for us* (see Phil 2:5-8).

The first time Jesus' vulnerability and weakness are linked to his role as king is at his birth. An angel tells his parents to name him Jesus, which means "salvation," because he will one day save his people from their sins (Mt 1:21). Although he was "God with us" (Is 7:14; Mt 1:23), he chose to take on the ultimate weakness—that of a newborn baby,

[8]For an extended discussion of this theme, see James M. Hamilton Jr., "The Skull Crushing Seed of the Woman: Inner-Biblical Interpretation of Genesis 3:15," *Southern Baptist Journal of Theology* 10, no. 2 (2006): 30-54.

[9]I first heard this turn of phrase from the ministry of H. B. Charles Jr.

who needed to be fed, changed, bathed, comforted, carried, and swaddled. In this newborn, God was entering the world and living among the very people he had created. Then in the very next scene, wise men come from the east, asking, "Where is he *who has been born king of the Jews?* For we saw his star when it rose and have come to worship him" (Mt 2:2, emphasis added). This weak baby will be a king who will accomplish salvation for his people.

Fast-forward thirty-three years to the night Jesus is betrayed. While one of his followers is willing to fight, Jesus tells him to put away his sword (Mt 26:51-52). Although he could call on legions of angels to save him, Jesus knows that his ultimate victory will come through ultimate weakness. He is delivered over for trial as king of the Jews (Mt 27:11), mocked and beaten as king of the Jews (Mt 27:27-31), and then nailed to a cross, with the charges on a sign above his head saying, "This is Jesus, the King of the Jews" (Mt 27:37). The crowd mocks, "He saved others; he cannot save himself. He is the King of Israel; let him come down now from the cross, and we will believe in him" (Mt 27:42).

After darkness comes upon the land for three hours, Jesus cries out with a loud voice, "My God, my God, why have you forsaken me?" (Mt 27:46). In that moment, King Jesus bears the wrath of God for our sin, and God the Father turns his face away from his beloved Son. Jesus cries out once again and yields up his spirit. The apostle Paul explains that in this moment, God the Father was putting his son, Jesus, forward as a *propitiation by his blood* (Rom 3:25)—"an offering that turns away the wrath of God directed against sin."[10] In the greatest moment of weakness and vulnerability in history, King Jesus *chose* to bear the wrath of God that our sins deserved, so that all who turn from their sins and trust his work are forgiven and reconciled to God: "In this is love, not that we have loved God but that he loved us and sent his Son to be the propitiation for our sins" (1 Jn 4:10).

---

[10]Stanley J. Grenz et al., *Pocket Dictionary of Theological Terms* (IVP Academic, 1999), 96.

While David's victory came in weakness, it was a military victory. Jesus' victory came in the ultimate display of *chosen* weakness, and it accomplished the ultimate victory—over sin, death, and hell *for us*. And just as the people of Israel could advance in the strength of David's victory to chase and rout the defeated foe, so Christians today live in light of the victory of Jesus that has been won for us. Like the Israelites, we don't fight *for* victory. We fight *from* victory. Because our eternal victory has been won by King Jesus, we live and serve Jesus with confidence that he will use us to continue to build his church until the day when every knee will bow at his throne, "in heaven and on earth and under the earth, and every tongue confess that Jesus Christ is Lord, to the glory of God the Father" (Phil 2:10-11). In the end, we *can* face giant obstacles in our lives—but not because of a pep talk such as, "You can do it, with God's help." We can face trials, temptations, threats, and anything else because Jesus has won the ultimate victory *for us*.

DISCUSSION QUESTIONS

1. Explain the concept of the king as the representative head of his people in your own words. Next, read Romans 5:12-21 out loud as a group and make observations about how this concept applies today, with Jesus as a perfect covenant head, in contrast to sinful Adam in Eden or sinful King David.
2. Read Deuteronomy 17:14-20 aloud as a group and list the various characteristics of Israel's anticipated, ideal king.
3. Read 1 Samuel 25 and 2 Samuel 3:1-5, 12-16; 5:13. Highlight how these passages hint at greater failures of David to come.
4. Why is 2 Samuel 6–7 the glory days of God's Old Testament people?
5. Why should the story of David and Goliath be applied as more than a pep talk that we can face giant challenges in our lives with God's help?

6. The chapter linked the weakness of Jesus to his role as King, both at his birth and at his death. Are there any other passages from Jesus' life that link the two? Think especially of passages where Jesus is presented as weak and vulnerable and also called either a king or the Son of David. Share with your group.

PROPHETS

PROCLAIMING YHWH'S WORD TO THE REDEEMED

WHEN WE HEAR THE WORD *PROPHET*, several images may come to mind. Maybe we think of a scam artist we have encountered, one who claims to have messages directly from God but leads people astray. Maybe we think of a John the Baptist figure: an eccentric, wise man of God with a mop of unkempt hair, a long beard, weird clothing, and an even weirder diet. Whatever (mis)conceptions we bring to this word, it is important to understand prophets in the Bible because they play a critical role in its story of redemption.

Many in the West take for granted that literacy is the norm and that we also have access to God's Word in numerous translations and formats. But before our glory days of having countless Bible translations in countless (and inexpensive) paper and digital formats, there was a famine of hearing the words of YHWH (see Amos 8:11). In biblical times, the Word of God was *being* written. It was not complete. In those days, the printing press was still thousands of years in the future, and even if there had been widespread access to the portions of God's Word that had been written, most people couldn't read. For these reasons, YHWH raised up and commissioned prophets.

Donald Fowler and Jason S. DeRouchie summarize the role of the Old Testament prophet:

> A prophet of Yahweh was a heavenly ambassador, who called Yahweh's people back to their covenant relationship with the Great King. When the prophet spoke, Yahweh spoke (Deut. 18:18), and because of this, history played out exactly how Yahweh's prophets said. "And the Lord . . . sent [bands of enemies] against Judah to destroy it, according to the word of the Lord that he spoke by his servants the prophets" (2 Kings 24:2). In 1–2 Kings, the prophets proclaimed the divine Word, acted with divine power (miracles), and combated wicked kings and disobedient Israelites.[1]

The Bible's prophets were mouthpieces of YHWH: They spoke his word to his redeemed people. Their prophetic messages were given by YHWH and were always aligned with the portions of the Bible that had already been written. Sometimes these messages were predictive: They foretold what YHWH would bring to pass in the future. More often, these messages simply brought YHWH's already-revealed truth to bear on a new life situation. Prophets were *forthtellers* of YHWH's word more often than they were *foretellers* of what YHWH would do in the future.

If we are going to understand the unfolding story of redemption in Joshua, Judges, Samuel, and Kings (and beyond), we need to explore what these books teach about prophets and their prophetic messages. We'll start by noticing that these four books *are* prophetic, we'll continue by exploring the prophets who appear in these books, and we'll close by looking forward to Christ as the greatest prophet the world has ever known.

JOSHUA, JUDGES, SAMUEL, AND KINGS ARE PROPHETIC BOOKS

In the present book's introduction we learned that Joshua, Judges, Samuel, and Kings appear in the Prophets section of the Hebrew

[1]Donald Fowler and Jason S. DeRouchie, "1–2 Kings," in *What the Old Testament Authors Really Cared About: A Survey of Jesus' Bible*, ed. Jason S. DeRouchie (Kregel Academic, 2013), 223.

Old Testament. One important reason for this is that all of these books "share a prophetic view of history in which cause and effect are tied to the blessings and curses of the covenant."[2] As we have noted, the Pentateuch concludes by promising blessings for covenant keeping, curses for covenant breaking, and restoration for covenant repentance (see Deut 28; 30:1-10; cf. Lev 26). These three headings act as a lens through which we can understand the rest of the Old Testament.

That is why this section of the Old Testament begins with a speech by YHWH to Joshua. As YHWH commissioned Joshua as Moses' successor, the one who would lead his people into the Promised Land, he guaranteed them success as long as they lived according to his instruction:

> Only be strong and very courageous, being careful to do according to all the law that Moses my servant commanded you. Do not turn from it to the right hand or to the left, that you may have good success wherever you go. This Book of the Law shall not depart from your mouth, but you shall meditate on it day and night, so that you may be careful to do according to all that is written in it. For then you will make your way prosperous, and then you will have good success. (Josh 1:7-8)

As long as his people kept his word, YHWH would give them success in taking the land, settling in the land, and living out their calling to bless all the families of the earth (see Gen 12:1-3).

In the Bible's story, YHWH is the main mover of history, and Israel succeeds or fails based on YHWH's favor or disfavor. For example, Judges 3 reports on a conflict between Moab and Israel. If it were reported as history in our day, it would read something like this: "King Eglon of Moab started to gain the upper hand in his conflict with Israel." That's it. But since Joshua, Judges, Samuel, and Kings share a

---

[2]Andrew E. Hill and John H. Walton, *A Survey of the Old Testament*, 4th ed. (Zondervan Academic, 2023), 140.

prophetic view of history, they tell the account of what happened through the lens of YHWH and his covenant with Israel. Here is the Bible's report: "And the people of Israel again did what was evil in the sight of the Lord, and the Lord strengthened Eglon the king of Moab against Israel, because they had done what was evil in the sight of the Lord" (Judg 3:12). The verse begins and ends with Israel doing evil in the sight of YHWH, with YHWH strengthening Israel's enemy against them sandwiched in between. Because Israel transgressed the covenant, YHWH set enemies against Israel to give them a taste of the covenant curses that would be theirs if they continued down this road.

JOSHUA, JUDGES, SAMUEL, AND KINGS TELL THE STORY OF NUMEROUS PROPHETS

In addition to being prophetic books, Joshua, Judges, Samuel, and Kings include many stories of prophets. Prior to these books, prophets appeared sporadically. For example, Moses is called the greatest prophet who has lived to that point in history (see Deut 34:10-12; cf. Num 12:6-7). Other prophets are Abraham (Gen 20:7), Aaron (Ex 7:1), and Miriam (a prophetess; Ex 15:20). On another occasion, seventy of Israel's elders prophesy, along with Eldad and Medad (Num 11:25-29). Finally, the pagan prophet Balaam is used by YHWH to report four oracles, the last of which speaks of the coming Messiah (Num 23–24).

The Old Testament story also reveals an alternative name for prophets that helps us understand how these figures received their messages. Learning this word also helps us identify a prophet in Scripture, who may be called by this alternative name. In 1 Samuel 9:9 we discover that prophets were originally called "seers" (see 2 Sam 24:11). This emphasizes that biblical prophets were given special visions into the divine realm. Let's read Balaam's most famous, messianic oracle and pay attention to how he received these words from God:

> The oracle of Balaam the son of Beor,
> the oracle of the man *whose eye is opened*,

> the oracle of him *who hears the words of God,*
> and knows the knowledge of the Most High,
> *who sees the vision of the Almighty,*
> falling down *with his eyes uncovered*:
> *I see him*, but not now;
> *I behold him*, but not near:
> a star shall come out of Jacob,
> and a scepter shall rise out of Israel;
> it shall crush the forehead of Moab
> and break down all the sons of Sheth.
> Edom shall be dispossessed;
> Seir also, his enemies, shall be dispossessed.
> Israel is doing valiantly.
> And one from Jacob shall exercise dominion
> and destroy the survivors of cities! (Num 24:15-19, emphasis added)

Of the six phrases I have emphasized with italics, five have to do with seeing and one with hearing. God gave Balaam a peek into the divine realm, and his prophetic message was the report of what he saw and heard.

In Joshua, Judges, Samuel, and Kings, numerous people appear who are called prophets, prophetesses, or seers, or who are said to prophesy or speak an oracle. Here they are:

Table 4.1. The unfolding story of prophets in Joshua, Judges, Samuel, and Kings

Prophet, Prophetess, Seer, One Who Prophesies, One Who Speaks an Oracle	Reference
Deborah	Judg 4:4
unnamed	Judg 6:8
Samuel	1 Sam 3:20; 9: 18-19
a group of prophets	1 Sam 10:5-13
King Saul	1 Sam 10:5-13; 19:23-24
the company of the prophets	1 Sam 19:20
messengers of Saul	1 Sam 19:20-21
Gad	1 Sam 22:5; 2 Sam 24:11

Prophet, Prophetess, Seer, One Who Prophesies, One Who Speaks an Oracle	Reference
Nathan	2 Sam 7:2; 12:25; 1 Kings 1:10-45
Zadok the priest	2 Sam 15:27
Ahijah	1 Kings 11:29; 14:2
an old prophet	1 Kings 13:11-32
a man of God	1 Kings 13:1-32
Jehu the son of Hanani	1 Kings 16:7, 12
the prophets of YHWH	1 Kings 18:4, 13
450 prophets of Baal and the 400 prophets of Asherah	1 Kings 18:19-40
Elijah	1 Kings 18:22, 36
Elisha	1 Kings 19:16; 2 Kings 3:11; 5:3-14; 6:12; 9:1
an unnamed prophet	1 Kings 20:13, 22
a man of the sons of the prophets	1 Kings 20:35, 38, 41
Zedekiah and the 400 lying prophets	1 Kings 22:6-23
Micaiah the son of Imlah	1 Kings 22:7-23
the sons of the prophets who were in Bethel	2 Kings 2:3-15; 4:1, 38; 5:22; 6:1; 9:1
the prophets of King Jehoram's father and mother	2 Kings 3:13
the prophets	2 Kings 9:7; 23:2
the prophets of Baal	2 Kings 10:19
Jonah the son of Amittai	2 Kings 14:25
every prophet and every seer; my servants the prophets	2 Kings 17:13, 23; 21:10; 24:2
Isaiah the son of Amoz	2 Kings 19:2; 20:1-14
Huldah the prophetess	2 Kings 22:14
the prophet who came out of Samaria	2 Kings 23:18

While prophets appear sporadically in the first five books of the Old Testament, by Joshua, Judges, Samuel, and Kings, they are more prominent. While some of these are pagan prophets (e.g., prophets of the Canaanite god Baal) and some are false prophets of YHWH (e.g., 1 Kings 22:6-23), many are authentic prophets who speak YHWH's word to his people.

The prophets section of the Hebrew Old Testament can be split in half: Joshua, Judges, Samuel, and Kings are the Former (or Speaking) Prophets, and Jeremiah, Ezekiel, Isaiah, and the Twelve are the Latter (or Writing) Prophets. In the Former Prophets, these prophetic figures *spoke* their message, and their ministries were recorded in the story of Joshua, Judges, Samuel, and Kings. In the Latter Prophets, these prophetic figures spoke their message as well, but their *words* were also recorded in entire books made up of their prophetic oracles. Paul House builds on what we have learned so far: "The Hebrew order [of Old Testament books] helps readers absorb the events from a prophetic viewpoint and then encounter the words the prophets themselves used to interpret the times in which they lived."[3]

Much more could be said about prophets. In 1–2 Samuel, the stories of the prophets Samuel and Nathan are told alongside the book's kings, Saul and David. In 1–2 Kings, the building of the temple and the stories of the prophets Elijah and Elisha are told in more detail and at greater length than most of the book's royal figures.[4] Whereas the kings in these books most often have their stories summarized briefly, the stories of Elijah and Elisha are the most prominent features of the middle third of these books: 1 Kings 17–2 Kings 13. Since Elijah and Elisha get so much attention in the book of Kings, they must be very important.[5]

For the rest of this chapter, we'll look at four attributes of the prophets who appear in Joshua, Judges, Samuel, and Kings. Then we will close by looking forward to Christ.

YHWH's word: To install kings. The rule of Israel's judges continues in the book of Samuel with Eli the priest (1 Sam 4:18) and then

---

[3]Paul R. House, *Old Testament Theology* (InterVarsity Press, 1998), 197.

[4]Because of space restrictions, and since there is so much overlap between the purpose of the temple and the tabernacle, I point readers to my earlier work on the important theme of the building of the tabernacle. See the chapter "Tabernacle, Priesthood, and Sacrifice: Provisions for the Redeemed," in Ian J. Vaillancourt, *The Dawning of Redemption: The Story of the Pentateuch and the Hope of the Gospel* (Crossway, 2022), 151-70.

[5]See Andreas J. Köstenberger and Gregory Goswell, *Biblical Theology: A Canonical, Thematic, and Ethical Approach* (Crossway, 2023), 185.

Samuel, who is also a judge (see 1 Sam 7:6, 15-17).[6] At first Samuel's miraculous birth may remind us of Samson, but (in contrast to Samson) his character is what sets him apart: "Now the boy Samuel continued to grow both in stature and in favor with the LORD and also with man" (1 Sam 2:26). In the words of Andrew E. Hill and John H. Walton, Samuel also becomes "YHWH's prophet, priest, and king-maker."[7] Waltke specifies: "In Israel [YHWH's] prophets designated the king: Samuel anointed Saul (1 Sam. 10:1) and David (16:1, 12-13); Nathan anointed Solomon (1 Kings 1:38-39); Ahijah designated Jeroboam (11:29-40), and so on. This function of the prophet terminates with John the Baptist, who designated Jesus of Nazareth as Messiah, Israel's long-awaited ideal, eschatological king."[8]

In this crucial period of Israel's history, when they are maturing from a loose association of tribes ruled by judges to a united nation ruled by a king, it makes sense that YHWH appoints prophets to identify and install Israel's kings.

YHWH's word: To shepherd and disturb kings. Since the leadership of Israel's king is to be shaped by YHWH's word (see Deut 17:14-20), prophets will be a great blessing—if the king listens.[9] Waltke explains: "The prophet represents [YHWH's] rule and covenant to the king. According to their words, kings and kingdoms come and go, the sick are healed or die. They oppose apostate kings by delivering specific pronouncements and/or deeds that apply the covenant's curses."[10] A vivid example of this is found in 1 Kings 22, where King

---

[6]In 1 Sam 8:1-9, Samuel briefly made his sons judges over Israel, but since they did not walk in his ways and since the people wanted a king, their authority in this regard was quickly replaced with the rule of King Saul.

[7]Hill and Walton, *Survey of the Old Testament*, 186.

[8]Bruce K. Waltke and Charles Yu, *An Old Testament Theology: An Exegetical, Canonical, and Thematic Approach* (Zondervan, 2007), 680.

[9]My former seminary professor summarized the role of the Old Testament prophet as loving God and disturbing people. See Donald A. Leggett, *Loving God and Disturbing Men: Preaching from the Prophets* (Baker, 1990). Anecdotally, Dr. Leggett shared with our class that his only regret in writing this book was the word *men* instead of *people* in its title.

[10]Waltke and Yu, *Old Testament Theology*, 750.

Ahab of Israel inquires for the word of YHWH about whether he and King Jehoshaphat of Judah should go to war against the Syrians (1 Kings 22:5). Four hundred false prophets are gathered and agree that the battle will be won (1 Kings 22:6). Jehoshaphat responds, "Is there not here another prophet of the LORD of whom we may inquire?" (1 Kings 22:7). Ahab replies, "There is yet one man by whom we may inquire of the LORD, Micaiah the son of Imlah, but I hate him, for he never prophesies good concerning me, but evil" (1 Kings 22:8).

As Ahab predicted, Micaiah's word from YHWH is vastly different from the other prophets: "I saw all Israel scattered on the mountains, as sheep that have no shepherd" (1 Kings 22:17). In other words, if they go to battle, they will lose. Ahab responds with exasperation: "Did I not tell you that he would not prophesy good concerning me, but evil?" (1 Kings 22:18). Ahab is clearly not interested in the truth; he wants to hear what he wants to hear.

Despite this opposition, the prophet explains further:

> Therefore hear the word of the LORD: I saw the LORD sitting on his throne, and all the host of heaven standing beside him on his right hand and on his left; and the LORD said, "Who will entice Ahab, that he may go up and fall at Ramoth-gilead?" And one said one thing, and another said another. Then a spirit came forward and stood before the LORD, saying, "I will entice him." And the LORD said to him, "By what means?" And he said, "I will go out, and will be a lying spirit in the mouth of all his prophets." And he said, "You are to entice him, and you shall succeed; go out and do so." Now therefore behold, the LORD has put a lying spirit in the mouth of all these your prophets; the LORD has declared disaster for you. (1 Kings 22:19-23)[11]

If the king over Israel or Judah knew what was best for him (and his nation!), he would listen to the message of Israel's faithful prophets. But too often he didn't, and this led to the persecution

---

[11]For a similar teaching in the New Testament, see 2 Thess 2:11-12.

and even murder of many prophets (e.g., 2 Kings 9:7). As disturbers of kings, the lives of YHWH's faithful prophets were often difficult (see Heb 11:32-38).

YHWH's pretenders: False prophets. We have just witnessed the frustration of Ahab when Micaiah would not tell him the message he wanted to hear. While many of Israel's prophets were faithful (and had the scars to prove it), others were false or lying prophets—such as the four hundred prophets who preceded Micaiah. As House puts it, "Each faction in Israel has prophets to argue its case. Prophets committed to Yahweh, Baal, Jeroboamism and sheer financial gain appear."[12] Far from being faithful, the false prophets were essentially "court functionaries on the king's payroll."[13]

How was a king to discern whether he would listen to a prophet? The earlier book of Deuteronomy provides a clear answer:

> If a prophet or a dreamer of dreams arises among you and gives you a sign or a wonder, and the sign or wonder that he tells you comes to pass, and if he says, "Let us go after other gods," which you have not known, "and let us serve them," you shall not listen to the words of that prophet or that dreamer of dreams. For the LORD your God is testing you, to know whether you love the LORD your God with all your heart and with all your soul. You shall walk after the LORD your God and fear him and keep his commandments and obey his voice, and you shall serve him and hold fast to him. But that prophet or that dreamer of dreams shall be put to death, because he has taught rebellion against the LORD your God, who brought you out of the land of Egypt and redeemed you out of the house of slavery, to make you leave the way in which the LORD your God commanded you to walk. So you shall purge the evil from your midst. (Deut 13:1-5)

Since false prophets were present, God's people (especially kings) needed to be discerning.

---

[12]House, *Old Testament Theology*, 259.
[13]House, *Old Testament Theology*, 261.

YHWH's power: To perform miracles. One reason prophets performed miracles was to show that divine power accompanied their message. Waltke explains:

> The prophets' credentials are their predictions and/or miracles. By these people know that there is a prophet in Israel (1 Kings 17:24; 22:28; 2 Kings 3:11; 5:8; 8:7-8). They authenticate their remote predictions by immediate signs (1 Kings 13:3-5; 14:12-16; 2 Kings 20:8-9; cf. Deut. 18:21-22). The full might of the God of Hosts is on their side for those with the spiritual sight to see (2 Kings 6:16).[14]

However, this was not foolproof, for false prophets could also summon supernatural power in an attempt to authenticate their false message (see Deut 13:1-5). Another reason prophets performed miracles, though, was to show YHWH's superiority over the false gods of Canaan.

Leila Leah Bronner has pointed out that the power of the Canaanite god Baal was celebrated with the motifs of fire, rain, oil and corn, child giving, healing, resurrection, ascent, and defeating the river god. Turning to the stories of Elijah and Elisha, she notices that YHWH displays his superiority over each of these areas:

> With regard to fire, Elijah defeats the prophets of Baal in a contest of fire on Mount Carmel (1 Kings 18:17-46; see also 1 Kings 19:12; 2 Kings 1:9-16; 2:11; 6:17). With regard to rain, Elijah begins his history-shaping ministry with the words: "There will be neither dew nor rain in the next few years except at my word" (1 Kings 17:1; cf. 1 Kings 18:41-46; 2 Kings 3:14-17; 7:1-2). With regard to food, [YHWH] feeds Elijah by the ravens (1 Kings 17:1-6; see also 1 Kings 17:7-16; 19:1-6; cf. 2 Kings 4:1-7, 42-44). With regard to child giving, Elisha grants the Shunammite woman a son (2 Kings 4:14-17). With regard to healing, Elisha heals Naaman (2 Kings 5:1-14; see also 4:18-36). With regard to resurrection, Elijah revives the woman of Zarephath's son (1 Kings 17:17-23; see also

[14]Waltke and Yu, *Old Testament Theology*, 750.

> 2 Kings 4:18-37; 13:20-21). With regard to the ascent motif, as Baal in the Baal myths mounts the clouds, Elijah goes up in a whirlwind (2 Kings 2:11). With regard to the River motif, the Ugaritic Baal epic said of Baal: "And a stick swooped in the hands of Baal, like an eagle between his fingers. It struck the head of Prince (Sea) twixt the eyes of Judge River: . . . destroyed Judge River." As a polemic against this myth, Elijah smites the Jordan and the river divides asunder (2 Kings 2:7-8; see also 2:14).[15]

In a context in which the evil dynasty of Omri is leading Israel into Baal worship, the miracles of these two remarkable prophets preach as loudly as their words: YHWH is the only true God.[16] Miracles authenticate their message *and* show YHWH to be more powerful than the false god Baal.

LOOKING FORWARD TO CHRIST: "LISTEN TO HIM!"

In his transfiguration, Jesus peeled back his glory for his closest followers to see (see Mt 17:1-13; Mk 9:1-13; Lk 9:28-36). In Matthew's account, this scene comes after Peter's confessing of Jesus as the Christ, Jesus' foretelling of his death and resurrection, and Jesus' teaching that his followers will need to take up their cross in order to follow him (Mt 16). Six days later, he leads Peter, James, and John up a high mountain by themselves. Jesus is then "transfigured before them, and his face shone like the sun, and his clothes became white as light" (Mt 17:2). While Moses' face shone in the Old Testament because he had encountered YHWH's glory, Jesus' face shines and his clothes become as white as light because of the glory that is inherent in himself.

Then another strange thing happens—Moses (the most prominent prophet of the Law) and Elijah (the most prominent prophet in the

---

[15]Waltke and Yu, *Old Testament Theology*, 746-747, summarizing Leila Leah Bronner, *The Stories of Elijah and Elisha as Polemics Against Baal Worship* (Brill, 1968).

[16]In fact, Elijah's name means "YHWH is my God."

Prophets) appear. Just as these prophets had powerful encounters with YHWH on mountains (Ex 3; 1 Kings 18:20-40), they are now on another mountain, talking with Jesus. In the middle of this scene, "a bright cloud overshadows them, and a voice from the cloud says, 'This is my beloved Son, with whom I am well pleased; *listen to him*'" (Mt 17:5, emphasis added). The bright cloud that overshadows them reminds us of the cloud of YHWH's glory in the story of Israel's exodus from Egypt, when God's people followed the cloud of his presence by day and the pillar of fire by night. This confirms that it is God speaking.

God calling Jesus his beloved Son sends our minds back to Genesis 22, where Abraham is willing to sacrifice his beloved son, Isaac. Could this be a hint at what will come next for God the Father's beloved Son?

In the context of our study of the Old Testament prophets, the last phrase is powerful: Moses, Elijah, Peter, James, and John are told to *listen to Jesus*. Moses and Elijah were the two most prominent prophets in the Old Testament, but in this scene they are to be silent because Jesus is the greater prophet. *Listen to him.*

Although at the time, Peter, James, and John were simply followers of Jesus, the first readers of Matthew's Gospel knew these men as pillars of the early church. All three of them went on to preach, write Scripture, and suffer greatly. Two of them even died for the gospel of Jesus Christ. In the presence of anyone else, they would have been the center of attention—the ones called on to speak in every crowd. That is, every crowd except this one. In the presence of Jesus, these future leaders of the church are called to keep silent and to focus on Jesus. *Listen to him.*

Jesus' disciples respond by falling on their faces in reverence and terror. As Jesus peels back his humanity and lets his glory shine forth, and as the voice of God the Father affirms Jesus in this scene, Peter, James, and John realize that when they are with Jesus, they are in the presence of God. Jesus comes and touches them, saying, "Rise, and have no fear" (Mt 17:7). The disciples lift up their eyes and see no one but Jesus.

Although the Bible records the lives of some incredible prophets, none of them compares to Jesus. In his presence, any other prophet need only be silent and *listen to him.*

All of this calls to mind Deuteronomy 18:18, where YHWH promises Moses, "I will raise up for them a prophet like you from among their brothers. And I will put my words in his mouth, and he shall speak to them all that I command him" (Deut 18:18). Coupled with the scene at the end of Deuteronomy, which says a prophet like Moses has not arisen since in Israel (Deut 34:10-12), this verse from the middle of Deuteronomy becomes a forward-looking promise. As careful readers of the Old Testament, we know that a prophet greater than Moses will come. Moses himself describes this coming prophet further: "The Lord your God will raise up for you a prophet like me from among you, from your brothers—*it is to him you shall listen*" (Deut 18:15, emphasis added). *Listen to him.* God the Father's words in Matthew 17:5 are linked with the hope expressed in Deuteronomy 18:15. On the Mount of Transfiguration, God's voice confirms that Jesus is the hoped-for prophet like Moses. Other prophets proclaimed awesome words, but none compared to his.

What are the words of Jesus to which we are called to listen? Surely this scene lends authority to the Sermon on the Mount—a link we will look at more closely in chapter eight. Surely through Jesus' life, demons and disease and even death *listened to him.* But what does Jesus say immediately after this scene? As they come down from the mountain together, Jesus speaks once more to Peter, James, and John: "Tell no one the vision, until the Son of Man is raised from the dead" (Mt 17:9). This not only looks ahead to Jesus' coming death and resurrection but also explains that the disciples are not to tell anyone about this incredible happening on the Mount of Transfiguration until after the key events of the gospel have taken place. This way, people will be able to understand its full significance.

As Jesus, Peter, James, and John walk down the mountain, they discuss John the Baptist as the hoped-for Elijah figure who was promised in Malachi 4:5. The disciples are told that, instead of listening to John the Baptist as the one sent to prepare the people to receive Jesus, the people did not listen to John or respect him as a prophet. In a way similar to how John the Baptist was mistreated by the Jews to whom he was sent, "So also the Son of Man will certainly suffer at their hands" (Mt 17:12). Before resurrection, Jesus tells them, there will be suffering. *Listen to him.*

Jesus was a great moral teacher and a miracle-worker filled with love and compassion, but his life was not summed up by these things. The central reason for his earthly existence is summed up in his death and resurrection—*listen to him* as he focuses our attention there. As the greatest prophet in history, Jesus proclaimed that he came to live the perfect life that all others had failed to live, to die the death under God's wrath that we deserved to die, and to rise from the dead, conquering death for us.[17] The purpose of his teaching, his miracles, his love and compassion, and other aspects of his life and ministry was to point to the most important thing: the gospel. Jesus is not merely a prophet who spoke the words of God; he is also the priest who offered the ultimate sacrifice for our sins. And—unlike Old Testament prophets, who merely spoke YHWH's word to kings—he is also the King who was raised from the dead and who today sits enthroned at the Father's right hand. What a Savior!

DISCUSSION QUESTIONS

1. Prior to reading this chapter, what was the first thought to come to your mind when you heard the word *prophet*?

---

[17]I first heard this wonderful gospel summary in the ministry of Tim Keller.

2. Why are the books of Joshua, Judges, Samuel, and Kings in the Prophets section of the Hebrew Old Testament? Give some examples of Bible passages that support your answer.
3. Read 1 Samuel 9:9. What older term had previously been used to designate a prophet, and how does this term help us to understand the role of the Old Testament prophet?
4. Share your favorite story from the accounts of Elijah and Elisha. How was your understanding of this story enhanced by the insights of Leila Leah Bronner (cited in this chapter)?
5. Did anything in the discussion of the Mount of Transfiguration stick out to you? Share with your group and give reasons for your answer.

5

DIVISION, DECLINE, AND EXILE

TRAGEDY FOR THE REDEEMED

After the robbery, one of the thieves notices a tiny cut on his wrist, but he ignores it and continues to celebrate with his partners in crime. As readers of a John Grisham novel, we anticipate what will come next after the presence of this little detail at the beginning of the story: the discovery of a drop of blood at the crime scene, an FBI database search for its DNA match, the identification of the ex-convict who had committed this crime, and a quick arrest.[1]

With literary mastery, Grisham zeroes in on a detail the story's readers and character both know. The character in the story should have known better, so all the extra, behind-the-scenes details find the reader shouting at a character who is walking into a trap. In this way, Grisham expertly contrasts an unsuspecting criminal who should have known better with an informed reader who can't wait to see how the FBI will get their man.

In a similar way, the book of Deuteronomy provides its characters and readers with vital information in the unfolding story of the Old Testament. YHWH redeemed his people after four hundred years of slavery in Egypt. And as the next generation is on the cusp of entering the land YHWH promised so long ago, he instructs Moses to write

[1]See the first chapter of John Grisham, *Camino Island* (Vintage, 2018).

Deuteronomy to prepare his redeemed to live faithfully to him *in the land*. As we have already seen, YHWH promises his people blessings if they will keep his covenant (Deut 28:1-16) and warns his people with curses if they break his covenant (Deut 28:17-68). Later, he instructs his people about what to do if they find themselves under the covenant curse: If they repent of their sins, they will be restored (Deut 30:1-10). Blessings for covenant keeping, curses for covenant breaking, and restoration for covenant repentance.[2]

As we have walked through the unfolding story of the Old Testament after the Pentateuch, we have noticed that the king has become the corporate head over YHWH's redeemed people. This means that a faithful, upright king will usher in YHWH's blessings for his covenant-keeping people. An unfaithful, evil king, however, will result in YHWH's curses on his covenant-breaking people.

Deuteronomy 28 and Deuteronomy 30:1-10 are an important lens through which we should read the unfolding story of redemption in the Old Testament Historical Books. In this chapter, we will unpack the story of redemption in the books of Kings under three headings: division, decline, and exile, all as tragedies for the redeemed.

DIVISION

In our chapter on kings, we didn't sugarcoat David's horrible failures, for the Bible doesn't. Like every hero in the Bible (other than Jesus), David had feet of clay. What set David apart as the greatest king in Israel's history, then, was not his perfection. It was his humility and his commitment to repentance. More than any other king in Israel's history, David resembled the model king outlined in Deuteronomy 17:14-20.[3] For this reason, as the book of

[2]These same three themes also appear in Lev 26. For a more thorough unpacking of these themes, see the chapter titled "Blessings and Curses: Warning the Redeemed," in Ian J. Vaillancourt, *The Dawning of Redemption: The Story of the Pentateuch and the Hope of the Gospel* (Crossway, 2022), 187-206.

[3]With the possible exception of Josiah in 2 Kings 22:2.

Kings unfolds, David is the standard against which the kings in his lineage are assessed.

Trouble will begin in the next generation, but Solomon's reign doesn't commence with problems. It begins with blessings. We noticed in chapter four that the prophets are given more prominence in the book of Kings than the monarchs themselves. But there is a second major emphasis in the book of Kings that also outstrips the stories of monarchs: the construction of the temple.

After the death of David, Solomon's reign begins extremely well, with his prayer for wisdom and examples of wise ruling (1 Kings 3), along with the blessing of YHWH over his reign (1 Kings 4). As Donald Fowler and Jason S. DeRouchie note, the beginning of this book is filled with fulfillments of YHWH's covenant with Abraham as it "opens by showing how Israel had become a massive nation (progeny/heirs) (1 Kings 4:20; cf. Gen. 22:17a), living in their land (1 Kings 4:21; cf. Gen. 15:18), ruled by kings (1 Kings 1:1; 4:1; etc.; cf. Gen. 17:6, 16), and blessing their neighbors (1 Kings 4:34; 10:1-13; Gen. 12:3)."[4] Four long chapters are devoted almost exclusively to the construction of the temple, its furnishings, and its dedication (1 Kings 5–8).[5] The ultimate symbol of settledness in a land with YHWH dwelling in their midst is finally accomplished as YHWH stops inhabiting a tent structure and his glory fills the Jerusalem temple (1 Kings 8:10-11).[6]

In many ways, that moment is the apex of the Old Testament story. David's reign was surely the glory days of God's people, but under Solomon the promise of settled rest in the land with YHWH dwelling in their midst is finally achieved. As promised in Deuteronomy 28, YHWH's people are abundantly lavished with blessings for covenant

[4]Donald Fowler and Jason S DeRouchie, "1–2 Kings," in *What the Old Testament Authors Really Cared About: A Survey of Jesus' Bible*, ed. Jason S. DeRouchie (Kregel Academic, 2013), 230.

[5]Of the 173 verses in these chapters, only 12 tell the story of Solomon's palace. The other 161 verses are focused on the Jerusalem temple.

[6]For a more thorough explanation of the tabernacle (with implications for the later Jerusalem temple), see the chapter titled "Tabernacle, Priesthood, and Sacrifice: Provisions for the Redeemed," in Vaillancourt, *Dawning of Redemption*, 151-70.

keeping. Here are just some of the blessings that God's people enjoyed at that time in their history:

> He will bless you in the land that the Lord your God is giving you. (Deut 28:8)
>
> The Lord will establish you as a people holy to himself, as he has sworn to you. (Deut 28:9)
>
> All the peoples of the earth shall see that you are called by the name of the Lord, and they shall be afraid of you. (Deut 28:10)

All of this is dependent, though, on one thing: "if you do not turn aside from any of the words that I command you today, to the right hand or to the left, to go after other gods to serve them" (Deut 28:14).

Tragically, just *three chapters* after this amazing high point, Solomon's heart is turned away from YHWH. In direct contrast to the portrait of the king in Deuteronomy 17:14-20, Solomon acquires riches and power and wives (e.g., 1 Kings 11:4). While David took multiple wives, Solomon's wives number in the hundreds (and his concubines in the thousands). And while David took a census of his army, Solomon acquires many horses for battle. In the end, Solomon's addiction to foreign women results in a spiritual double-mindedness that pulls his heart away from YHWH.[7] In contrast to sinful yet repentant David, Solomon's turning away from faithfulness to YHWH is not corrected by repentance. As Waltke puts it, "the wisest man who ever lived before Jesus Christ (3:12) dies a fool because he stopped listening to instruction (Prov. 19:27)."[8]

In contrast to the considerable focus on the temple in 1 Kings 5–8, after Solomon turns his heart away from YHWH in 1 Kings 11, the temple isn't

---

[7]See Bruce K. Waltke and Charles Yu, *An Old Testament Theology: An Exegetical, Canonical, and Thematic Approach* (Zondervan, 2007), 704. The problem with Solomon's marriages to foreign women was not racial: It was, first, that he married more than one wife, and, second, that these non-Israelite wives were idol worshipers, so they turned his heart away from YHWH and to their gods.

[8]Waltke and Yu, *Old Testament Theology*, 706.

mentioned in the following eighteen chapters. What was the most significant accomplishment in Solomon's reign is now simply ignored by the author of Kings. Instead, we read story after story of idolatry.[9]

Because of the royal and national abandonment of YHWH, the kingdom is split in two after Solomon's death, with Israel in the north and Judah in the south (1 Kings 11–12). Solomon's son Rehoboam reigns in the south, and Jeroboam (the son of Solomon's servant; 1 Kings 11:26) reigns in the north (see 1 Kings 11–14). For the rest of Kings, the kingdom continues to be divided, and the king's (and people's) heart grows more distant from YHWH.

The division of the kingdom into Israel in the north and Judah in the south was *tragic*, and it was the first step toward even greater tragedies to come. Israel had experienced the exodus from Egypt, and after a forty-year wait, they had *finally* begun to inhabit the Promised Land. After the period of the judges, they had *finally* matured "from an association of twelve tribes into a fully formed nation."[10] Under Saul, and then David and Solomon, they *finally* experienced national unity, with a capital city in Jerusalem and the temple as a permanent place for YHWH to dwell among his people. But this lasted only for the reigns of the first three kings. After 650 years in the Promised Land, everything the Old Testament had been building toward was beginning to fall apart.[11] But the end was just beginning.

DECLINE

In line with Deuteronomy 28:15-68, the next horrible part of the story comes with the spiritual and political decline of the divided kingdom. The rest of the book of Kings tells the story of Israel in the north and

[9]I was first alerted to the absence of mentions of the temple after 1 Kings 11 in Oren Martin, *Bound for the Promised Land*, New Studies in Biblical Theology 34 (IVP Academic, 2015), 93-94.

[10]David J. H. Beldman, *Deserting the King: The Book of Judges* (Lexham, 2017), 2.

[11]For the number 650, see Waldemar Janzen, "Geography of Faith: A Christian Perspective on the Meaning of Places," *Studies in Religion* 3, no. 2 (1973): 166-82, as cited in Stephen G. Dempster, *Dominion and Dynasty: A Theology of the Hebrew Bible*, New Studies in Biblical Theology 15 (InterVarsity Press, 2003), 126.

Judah in the south with an eye on their kings. As we saw in our chapter on the Old Testament kings, this is because of the corporate solidarity between the king and his people in the Old Testament. In this section, there are some stories of events from the lives of individual kings, but the emphasis—and the structure of the whole—is on the beginning and end of each king's reign.

My wife and I once spent a day canoeing downstream on a slowly moving river. The rental place drove us for a short trip upstream, but we soon found that the twenty-eight-kilometer (17.4-mile) trip felt much longer than the drive. When we checked a map that night, we noticed that the Grand River twists and turns and snakes around. The drive to our drop-off point was short because it was *straight*, but on the river it was a much farther distance to our car. We ultimately ended up downstream, but it took us much longer to get there than we thought it should have.

The story of 1 Kings 12–2 Kings 25 is a lot like this canoeing experience. The spiritual, moral, and political decline of Israel and Judah lead the story *down, down, down.* But because of some bright spots along the way, the trip downstream into sin and decline was not as direct as it might have been. For example, King Josiah is said to have done what was right in the eyes of YHWH, walking in the way of his ancestor, David, not turning aside to the right or the left (2 Kings 22:2; cf. Deut 17:20).

The author of Kings crafts his story by alternating between accounts of the kings of Israel and those of Judah. In each case, the king and his kingdom are named. The king's father is also identified, and in the case of Judah's kings, his mother is named. The beginning of each king's reign is told with reference to the king of the other kingdom. For example, King Jehoshaphat of Judah begins his reign in the fourth year of King Ahab of Israel (1 Kings 22:41-44). Most crucially, an assessment of the king's reign is given, whether he was evil or upright, followed by a summary of his reign at the end of his life.

All of the kings of Israel in the north are said to have been evil. Andreas Köstenberger and Gregory Goswell summarize the situation in the Southern Kingdom of Judah:

> In the regnal formulae, the good (only southern) kings are those who do what is "right in the eyes of YHWH," of whom there are only eight: Asa, Jehoshaphat, Jehoash, Amaziah, Azariah, Jotham, Hezekiah, and Josiah (1 Kings 15:11; 22:43; 2 Kings 12:2; 14:3; 15:3, 34; 18:3; 22:2). However, only three kings reach such a level that they are likened to David, the prototypical good king (Asa, Hezekiah, Josiah). Both Hezekiah and Josiah are praised by being said to be incomparable (2 Kings 18:5; 23:25), and in line with this high commendation, Hezekiah is not merely said to be like David (as stated of Asa), but that he did "all that David his father had done" (2 Kings 18:3). However, the description of Josiah is the most impressive, for "[he] walked in all the way of David his father, and he did not turn aside to the right hand or to the left" (2 Kings 22:2).[12]

Table 5.1 summarizes the story of the kings of the divided kingdom:

Table 5.1. The unfolding story of kings of the divided kingdom

Monarch	Kingdom	Parents	Began in . . .	Duration	Assessment	Reign Began	Reign Ended
Jeroboam	Israel	Nebat (servant of Solomon) and Zeruah	—	22 years	evil	1 Kings 11:26; 12:20	1 Kings 14:19-20
Rehoboam	Judah	Solomon and Naamah the Ammonite	—	17 years	Judah did evil	1 Kings 11:43; 14:21	1 Kings 14:29-31
Abijam	Judah	Rehoboam and Maacah daughter of Abishalom	eighteenth year of Jeroboam	3 years	evil	1 Kings 15:1-2	1 Kings 15:7-8
Asa	Judah	Abijam and Maacah daughter of Abishalom	twentieth year of Jeroboam	41 years	upright, with some omissions	1 Kings 15:9-15	1 Kings 15:23-24

[12]Andreas J. Köstenberger and Gregory Goswell, *Biblical Theology: A Canonical, Thematic, and Ethical Approach* (Crossway, 2023), 186.

Monarch	Kingdom	Parents	Began in . . .	Duration	Assessment	Reign Began	Reign Ended
Nadab	Israel	Jeroboam	second year of Asa	2 years	evil	1 Kings 15:25-26	1 Kings 15:31-32
Baasha	Israel	Ahijah	third year of Asa	24 years	evil	1 Kings 15:33-34	1 Kings 16:5-6
Elah	Israel	Baasha	twenty-sixth year of Asa	2 years	evil	1 Kings 16:8	1 Kings 16:14
Zimri	Israel	—	twenty-seventh year of Asa	7 days	evil	1 Kings 16:10	1 Kings 16:20
Omri	Israel	—	thirty-first year of Asa	12 years (6 in Tirzah)	evil	1 Kings 16:23-26	1 Kings 16:27-28
Ahab	Israel	Omri	thirty-eighth year of Asa	22 years	very evil	1 Kings 16:29-30	1 Kings 22:39
Jehoshaphat	Judah	Asa and Azubah	fourth year of Ahab	25 years	upright, with some omissions	1 Kings 22:41-44	1 Kings 22:45-50
Ahaziah	Israel	Ahab	seventeenth year of Jehoshaphat	2 years	evil	1 Kings 22:51-53	2 Kings 1:18
Jehoram (or Joram)	Israel	Ahab	eighteenth year of Jehoshaphat	12 years	evil	2 Kings 3:1-3	2 Kings 9:24
Jehoram (or Joram)	Judah	Jehoshaphat	fifth year of Joram (Jehoram)	8 years	evil	2 Kings 8:16-19	2 Kings 8:23-24
Ahaziah	Judah	Jehoram and Athaliah, granddaughter of Omni king of Israel	twelfth year of Joram	1 year	evil	2 Kings 8:25-27	2 Kings 9:27-28
Jehu	Israel	Jehoshaphat	—	28 years	evil	2 Kings 9:1-10	2 Kings 10:34-36
Athaliah mother of Ahaziah	Judah	granddaughter of Omni king of Israel	—	6 years	evil	2 Kings 11:1-3	2 Kings 11:13-16
Joash (also Jehoash)	Judah	Ahaziah and Zibiah of Beersheba	seventh year of Jehu	40 years	upright, with some omissions	2 Kings 11:21–12:3	2 Kings 12:19-21
Jehoahaz (or Joahaz)	Israel	Jehu	twenty-third year of Joash	17 years	evil	2 Kings 13:1-2	2 Kings 13:8-9

Monarch	Kingdom	Parents	Began in . . .	Duration	Assessment	Reign Began	Reign Ended
Jehoash (also Joash)	Israel	Jehoahaz	thirty-seventh year of Joash	16 years	evil	2 Kings 13:10-11	2 Kings 13:12-13; 14:15-16
Amaziah	Judah	Joash and Jehoaddin of Jerusalem	second year of Joash	29 years	upright, with some omissions	2 Kings 14:1-4	2 Kings 14:18-20
Jeroboam	Israel	Joash	fifteenth year of Amaziah	41 years	evil	2 Kings 14:23-24	2 Kings 14:28-29
Azariah (or Uzziah)	Judah	Amaziah and Jecoliah of Jerusalem	twenty-seventh year of Jeroboam	52 years	upright, with some omissions	2 Kings 15:1-4	2 Kings 15:6-7
Zechariah	Israel	Jeroboam	thirty-eighth year of Azariah	6 months	evil	2 Kings 15:8-9	2 Kings 15:11
Shallum	Israel	Jabesh	thirty-ninth year of Uzziah (or Azariah)	1 month	—	2 Kings 15:13	2 Kings 15:15
Menahem	Israel	Gadi	thirty-ninth year of Azariah (or Uzziah)	10 years	evil	2 Kings 15:17-18	2 Kings 15:21-22
Pekahiah	Israel	Menahem	fiftieth year of Azariah (or Uzziah)	2 years	evil	2 Kings 15:23-24	2 Kings 15:26
Pekah	Israel	Remaliah	fifty-second year of Azariah (or Uzziah)	20 years	evil	2 Kings 15:27-28	2 Kings 15:30-31
Jotham	Judah	Uzziah (or Azariah) and Jerusha daughter of Zadok	second year of Pekah	16 years	upright, with some omissions	2 Kings 15:32-35	2 Kings 15:36-38
Ahaz	Judah	Jotham	seventeenth year of Pekah	16 years	evil	2 Kings 16:1-4	2 Kings 16:19-20
Hoshea	Israel	Elah	twelfth year of Ahaz	9 years	evil	2 Kings 17:1-2	Assyrian exile in 2 Kings 17:6-23

Monarch	Kingdom	Parents	Began in . . .	Duration	Assessment	Reign Began	Reign Ended
Hezekiah	Judah	Ahaz	third year of Hoshea	29 years	upright	2 Kings 18:1-8	2 Kings 20:20-21
Manasseh	Judah	Hezekiah and Hephzibah	—	55 years	evil	2 Kings 21:1-2	2 Kings 21:17-18
Amon	Judah	Manasseh and Meshullemeth daughter of Haruz of Jotbah	—	2 years	evil	2 Kings 21:19-20	2 Kings 21:25-26
Josiah	Judah	Amon and Jedidah daughter of Adaiah of Bozkath	—	31 years	upright	2 Kings 22:1-2	2 Kings 23:28-30
Jehoahaz	Judah	Josiah and Hamutal daughter of Jeremiah of Libnah	—	3 months	evil	2 Kings 23:31-32	2 Kings 23:33-35
Jehoiakim (or Eliakim)	Judah	Josiah and Zebidah daughter of Pedaiah of Ruma	—	11 years	evil	2 Kings 23:36-37	2 Kings 24:5-6
Jehoiachin	Judah	Jehoiakim and Nehushta daughter of Elnathan of Jerusalem	—	3 months	evil	2 Kings 24:8-9	first wave of Babylonian exile in 2 Kings 24:10-17
Zedekiah (or Mattaniah)	Judah	(Josiah?) and Hamutal daughter of Jeremiah of Libnah	—	11 years	evil	2 Kings 24:18-20	Babylonian exile in 2 Kings 25:1-30

Once again, the trajectory was *down*, but the presence of eight upright kings in the Southern Kingdom of Judah slowed the rate of decline. Waltke explains further:

> The presence of the Davidic covenant in Judah and its absence in the north explains why the kingship in the north was plagued with

> instability and violence in contrast to the south. In the northern kingdom, twenty rulers represented nine different dynasties during the approximately 210 years from the division of the northern kingdom in 930 BC until the fall of Samaria in 722–21. Eight were put to death by usurpers, one fell in battle, one died in an accident. In the south there were also twenty kings, but these were all descended from David and spanned a period of 345 years, from 930 to the fall of Jerusalem in 586.[13]

While the decline took longer for Judah, the story of Israel and Judah both ended downstream at the same destination: exile.

EXILE

I began this chapter with a scene from a John Grisham novel, and my point was that the story's character should have known what was coming. Something similar was true for God's Old Testament people, for they knew their covenant breaking would ultimately result in exile: "The Lord will bring you and your king whom you set over you to a nation that neither you nor your fathers have known. And there you shall serve other gods of wood and stone. And you shall become a horror, a proverb, and a byword among all the peoples where the Lord will lead you away" (Deut 28:36-37; cf., e.g., 2 Kings 21:10-15). Once again, the reason for this tragedy was also made clear: "All these curses shall come upon you and pursue you and overtake you till you are destroyed, because you did not obey the voice of the Lord your God, to keep his commandments and his statutes that he commanded you" (Deut 28:45). In light of the downward trajectory of the book of Kings, disaster was clearly looming.

First, the Assyrian army defeated the Northern Kingdom of Israel in 722 BC and carried many of its survivors into exile. Then, as the next world superpower, the Babylonian army performed numerous invasions of Judah in the south until the temple was finally destroyed

[13]Waltke and Yu, *Old Testament Theology*, 752.

and the last wave of exiles was removed in 587/586 BC. By the end of the book of Kings, God's people had been carried away from the Promised Land, the temple was destroyed, and there was no king on David's throne. As Oren Martin puts it, "If the glorious part of Israel's history is her reception of the land, the tragedy is that this gift was forfeited. In Israel's history, then, just as the exodus served as the paradigmatic event of redemption, so the exile represented the paradigmatic event of judgment."[14] In fact, as we look back in the Bible's story, the exile of Israel sounds like Adam and Eve's banishment from the garden of Eden: The sin of the people resulted in their banishment from God's special place, where he had dwelled among them. The curses for covenant breaking had come on God's people, and they were desperate.

If God's people did not have in their Bible the promise of restoration for covenant repentance, there would have been no hope. Deuteronomy 30:1-10 instructs them what to do if they find themselves suffering in exile under the wrath of YHWH: They are to turn to the very one whose wrath they are enduring. According to the prophet Jeremiah, this restoration will not begin for another seventy years (Jer 29:10-14). The book of Kings ends, therefore, in the tragedy of exile, along with a tiny glimmer of hope. After King Zedekiah is removed from the throne, he sees his sons executed and has his eyes gouged out (2 Kings 25:7). We might be tempted to think that all is lost, but it is not. At the very end of the story, King "Jehoiachin is yet alive and well. Symbolically his prison clothing is removed (cf. Lev. 16:4, 32; Zech. 3:1-7), and he is given a seat of honor higher than the other captive kings" (2 Kings 25:27-30).[15] In the face of tragedy, this glimmer of hope was all God's people had. Even with so many losses, they were still being pointed to a coming Messiah.[16]

---

[14]Martin, *Bound for the Promised Land*, 100-101.

[15]Waltke and Yu, *Old Testament Theology*, 737.

[16]See Waltke and Yu, *Old Testament Theology*, 752.

Before we look forward from the story of Kings to Christ, we need to circle back to an insight from this book's introduction. According to the earliest attested Hebrew order of Old Testament books, the Bible's story of redemption is paused after the division, decline, and exile experienced in the book of Kings. In the books that follow, Jeremiah, Ezekiel, Isaiah, and the Twelve (Minor Prophets) will speak their prophetic messages to YHWH's exiled people. In those books, YHWH's people will learn how they got there, how they can come back to YHWH, and of YHWH's awesome plan to send a Savior who will fulfill the entire Old Testament hope. The book of Kings ends in tension, but the Latter (Writing) Prophets will speak into that tension with a call to repentance and a message of ultimate hope.

LOOKING FORWARD TO CHRIST: THE EXILE AND WILDERNESS EXPERIENCE OF JESUS

When we read the four Gospels, it is easy for us to focus on what we rightly think are the high points: Jesus' birth, baptism, Sermon on the Mount, miracles, triumphal entry, death, and resurrection. When we begin to go deeper and spend time noticing some of the other elements of the story, we discover even more wonderful truths. As I have been modeling in this book, this is especially the case as we approach the New Testament with a deeper understanding of the Old Testament. When we read the Gospel of Matthew with the division, decline, and exile of God's Old Testament people in our minds, we discover the exile and wilderness experience of Jesus.

After Jesus' miraculous birth and the visit of the wise men, "an angel of the Lord appeared to Joseph in a dream and said, 'Rise, take the child and his mother, and *flee to Egypt*, and remain there until I tell you, for Herod is about to search for the child, to destroy him'" (Mt 2:13, emphasis added). This detail sounds horrible: Jesus and his family had to flee to Egypt while Herod murdered every male child two years old or younger in Bethlehem and its surrounding region

(Mt 2:14, 16). It wasn't until the death of Herod that Joseph, Mary, and Jesus could return from Egypt to the land of Israel (Mt 2:21).

When we read these details with our minds filled with the Old Testament story, new connections spring from the page. In this case, we find a clear echo of Israel's exodus from Egypt (Ex 1–18). Matthew makes this connection clear when he says, "This was to fulfill what the Lord had spoken by the prophet, 'Out of Egypt I called my son'" (Mt 2:15, citing Hos 11:1). As we turn back to this Old Testament passage, we discover that Hosea 11:1 is not a prophecy about a singular son of YHWH. It is a prophecy about the *nation of Israel* as the collective son of YHWH. Why does Matthew claim this was fulfilled by Jesus' exile and return? The answer becomes clear when we learn a broader principle in the New Testament: Jesus embodies Israel. He was the perfect man who was sent into a sinful world to experience everything Israel experienced. But where Israel had failed, Jesus succeeded. And Jesus succeeded *for us*. This means that in his flight to Egypt, wait in Egypt, and return to Israel, Jesus was embodying the experience of God's Old Testament people in their flight to Egypt during a famine, four hundred years of slavery in Egypt, and exodus from Egypt to the Promised Land. Since the prophets spoke of the true and ultimate return from Babylonian exile in exodus-like terms (e.g., Is 11–12), the exodus of Jesus in Matthew 2 fulfilled this prophecy. The ultimate redemption was about to be fully accomplished through Jesus.

After his return, Jesus is baptized by John the Baptist. Why would sinless Jesus participate in this ceremony that focused on crowds of people confessing their sins and being baptized by John in the Jordan River (Mt 3:6)? Apparently, John has the same question, and he exclaims, "I need to be baptized by you, and do you come to me?" (Mt 3:14). Jesus replies, "Thus it is fitting for us to fulfill all righteousness" (Mt 3:15). This means that in his baptism, Jesus is once again identifying with sinful Israel, anticipating the cross, where he will take the sin of the world on himself. In contrast to sinful Israel, a voice from heaven responds to Jesus' baptism with words of absolute affirmation: "This is my beloved Son, with whom I am well pleased" (Mt 3:17). There was no sin in Jesus.

Immediately after his baptism, we learn that "Jesus was led up by the Spirit into the wilderness to be tempted by the devil" (Mt 4:1). Another wilderness experience. While Jesus' first wilderness experience happened in his infancy, this one occurred as his public ministry was about to begin. Jesus fasted forty days and nights—an echo of the forty years of wilderness wandering of Israel in the book of Numbers. Then he endured three separate temptations by the devil. In his state of absolute hunger, the temptations would have been all the more enticing. As the author of Hebrews puts it, "We do not have a high priest who is unable to sympathize with our weaknesses, but one who in every respect has been tempted as we are, yet without sin" (Heb 4:15). In fact, since Jesus *never* sinned, we can conclude that he felt temptations to a greater degree than we do because he resisted them entirely.

Each time the devil tempts Jesus, Jesus rebuffs him with the Word of God—a reminder of how important it is for Christians to fill their minds with Scripture. Jesus cites three different passages from Deuteronomy, reinforcing the importance of being *whole-Bible Christians* who immerse ourselves in the Old Testament as much as the New Testament. The devil entices Jesus in one of the temptations by quoting (and intentionally misapplying) Scripture, reinforcing the need for Christians to seriously pursue a proper, ever-deepening understanding of God's Word.

As we step back and survey these exile and wilderness experiences of Jesus, a precious truth stands out: By embodying Israel in these experiences, Jesus succeeded where Israel had failed. Israel was tested in their wilderness experiences and found to be sinful. Jesus was tested in his wilderness experience and found to be the faithful Son of God. Although Christians rightly emphasize the death of Jesus for our sins, we sometimes forget to revel in what theologians call his *active obedience*. This doctrine reminds us that Jesus was not merely the Son of God who was born perfect and then died for our sins. Jesus also faced *real temptations*, and he never sinned. He obeyed where every other human being in history failed. Jesus could not have been the perfect sacrifice apart from his obedience on our behalf. Israel's division, decline, and exile resulted from their sin. Jesus' exile and wilderness experiences resulted from his mission—to succeed *for us* and then experience the ultimate exile from God's presence on the cross as he took our sins on himself and died *for us*. And he did this so our eternity would be the opposite of exile. What a glorious gospel.

DISCUSSION QUESTIONS

1. How does Deuteronomy 28; 30:1-10 act as an essential lens through which we can understand the book of Kings?
2. Why is the construction and dedication of the temple given so much attention in 1 Kings 5–8?
3. Read Deuteronomy 17:14-20. In what ways does this passage alert us to the downfall of King Solomon that will come in 2 Kings 11?
4. How does this chapter's story of a canoe trip on a river help to make sense of 1 Kings 12–2 Kings 25?
5. Look at the chart of the kings of the divided kingdom and read aloud each king, his kingdom, and assessment (evil or upright). Do you notice a pattern in the north that is different from the south? What is it?
6. Why was the exile more than simply a political tragedy but also a spiritual one?
7. How did Jesus' life guarantee that Christians will experience an eternity that is the opposite of exile?

6

INGRAFTING

EXTENDING THE REDEEMED

Cultivating an olive crop takes work. As a person is trained to nurture an orchard, though, these trees can thrive and produce a bumper crop of olives that yield lots of olive oil. While the uninitiated may not know what to do with failing plants, the master horticulturalist can revive a failing orchard, partly through the practice of grafting. A popular dictionary defines grafting as "a shoot or bud of one plant that is inserted into or joined to the stem, branch, or root of another plant so that the two grow together as a single plant."[1] When this happens, a small part of an unhealthy, underproducing olive tree can be grafted into the trunk of a healthy, thriving olive tree. Over time, the two plants will become one, and the part from the unhealthy tree will thrive because it draws its nutrients from the root system of the healthy tree.

Throughout the Bible, we learn that God's goal was never to redeem a single people group. Beginning with Israel, he had the ultimate goal of grafting non-Jews into a covenant relationship with YHWH. In this chapter, we'll begin by tracing the theme of ingrafting in the Old Testament story, and then we'll focus our attention on the book of Ruth and the significance of its place as first in the Writings. We'll close by

[1]"Graft," Dictionary.com, www.dictionary.com/browse/graft.

looking forward to Christ and the impact his work has had on the redemption of non-Jews.

THE PROMISE OF INGRAFTING

Genesis 12 marks a significant turning point in the Bible's story. In the call of Abram, YHWH's plan of redemption gets very specific: He calls one man and promises that this man's descendants will be his special people. For this reason, the rest of the Old Testament story is focused on the growth of Abraham's descendants into YHWH's special people, Israel.

As we look closer at Genesis 12, though, we also find the promise of a global future. Let's read it carefully:

> Now the LORD said to Abram, "Go from your country and your kindred and your father's house to the land that I will show you. And I will make of you a great nation, and I will bless you and make your name great, so that you will be a blessing. I will bless those who bless you, and him who dishonors you I will curse, *and in you all the families of the earth shall be blessed*." (Gen 12:1-3, emphasis added)[2]

We have already summarized most of this passage: Abram was called by YHWH, and YHWH promised to make him into a great nation. But what about the very last clause? When YHWH adds, "in you all the families of the earth shall be blessed," he reveals that getting specific—with one nation as his special people—has an end goal: that all the families of the earth will be blessed in this nation. In this context, YHWH is not merely saying that all the families of the earth will be blessed with an easy life. He is saying that they will *become his people*. They will be *grafted into the descendants of Abraham*. This means that as YHWH is zeroing in on one man and his descendants, he is also revealing his endgame: that his special people will be

[2]For a helpful outline of this passage, along with a compelling translation, see Peter J. Gentry and Stephen J. Wellum, *Kingdom Through Covenant: A Biblical-Theological Understanding of the Covenants*, 2nd ed. (Crossway, 2018), 267.

multiethnic and global. In fact, his end goal is a special people that would include every single world ethnicity.

This means that as we read the Bible, we should be looking for ways ingrafting is beginning to unfold. The first hint comes in the immediate context of Genesis 12. At the Tower of Babel, languages, ethnicities, and global inhabitation are the result of *sin* (Gen 11:1-9). But though YHWH judges these prideful people by scattering them over the face of all the earth, in the next chapter—specifically Genesis 12:3—he looks ahead to a future when these very people groups will be blessed in Abram. YHWH's judgment at Babel is quickly followed with his plan to bless those same peoples.

As we scan the unfolding story of the Old Testament we discover several instances of non-Jews finding blessing in the descendants of Abraham. But for the sake of space, we'll look briefly at two examples before unpacking a third more thoroughly. The first is the unlikeliest of converts: a Canaanite sex worker. When Joshua sends twelve spies into the city of Jericho in the land of Canaan, a prostitute named Rahab houses them, hides them, believes that YHWH will give them the land, and confesses, "for the Lord your God, he is God in the heavens above and on the earth beneath" (Josh 2:11). When Joshua leads Israel into battle with Jericho, Rahab and her family are spared, and they are incorporated into Israel (Josh 6). *Rahab was grafted into Israel.*

Our next scene takes place much later in Israel's history. When the queen of Sheba visits King Solomon, she encounters his wisdom and his prosperity, and "there was no more breath in her" (1 Kings 10:5). Then she confesses, "Blessed be the Lord your God, who has delighted in you and set you on the throne of Israel! Because the Lord loved Israel forever, he has made you king, that you may execute justice and righteousness" (1 Kings 10:9). This non-Jewish queen confesses that all of Solomon's blessings have come from YHWH, from his delight in Solomon and his love for Israel. Although the Bible does not reveal whether she was grafted into Israel as a convert, this scene is at least a foretaste of all the families of the earth being blessed in the descendants of Abraham.

THE INGRAFTING OF RUTH

Our third example deserves more attention because not only does the book of Ruth showcase an incredible example of a non-Jew's grafting into Israel, but this book's placement in the Hebrew Old Testament hints at something far-reaching.

Ruth's conversion. The book of Ruth begins with a famine in Bethlehem, a town name that means "house of bread."[3] This place of abundant food has turned into a place of starvation. It is possible that the book's setting—at the time when the judges ruled (Ruth 1:1)—hints toward the reason for such a famine: the disobedience of YHWH's people. In response to this famine, a couple named Elimelech and Naomi sojourn to the country of Moab, along with their two sons, Mahlon and Chilion. In Moab, Elimelech dies, and his two sons marry Moabite wives named Orpah and Ruth. Ten years later, the two sons also die, leaving a grieving mother/widow living away from home with two foreign daughters-in-law (Ruth 1:1-5).

On the surface this scene is tragic, but we need to remember that YHWH clearly commanded his people not to marry outside Israel so that their hearts would not be pulled to worship idols, and Orpah and Ruth are idol-worshiping Moabite women. As Köstenberger and Goswell put it, "Ruth's designation as 'the Moabitess' is found seven times in the book (1:4, 22; 2:2, 6, 21; 4:5, 10), highlighting her outsider status."[4] When Naomi hears that YHWH visited his people and made Bethlehem ("the house of bread") abundant again, she and her two daughters-in-law begin their journey. Early in their trip, though,

---

[3]The Hebrew word *beth* means "house," and the Hebrew word *lehem* means "bread."

[4]Andreas J. Köstenberger and Gregory Goswell, *Biblical Theology: A Canonical, Thematic, and Ethical Approach* (Crossway, 2023), 298.

Naomi tells them to go back home and remarry. But Orpah and Ruth want to stay with her (Ruth 1:6-10).

The book of Deuteronomy helps us to understand what comes next:

> If brothers dwell together, and one of them dies and has no son, the wife of the dead man shall not be married outside the family to a stranger. Her husband's brother shall go in to her and take her as his wife and perform the duty of a husband's brother to her. And the first son whom she bears shall succeed to the name of his dead brother, that his name may not be blotted out of Israel. (Deut 25:5-6)

In her conversation with Orpah and Ruth, Naomi points out that she doesn't have any more sons for them to marry. She is also old, and even if she could have a son, it would take a long time for him to get to a marriageable age (Ruth 1:11-13). Orpah kisses Naomi goodbye and goes back home, but Ruth decides to stay (Ruth 1:14).

What happens next makes clear that these were religious decisions. Naomi commends Orpah for going back to her people *and her gods* (Ruth 1:15), but Ruth resolves differently: "Do not urge me to leave you or to return from following you. For where you go I will go, and where you lodge I will lodge. Your people shall be my people, *and your God my God*. Where you die I will die, and there will I be buried. May the Lord do so to me and more also if anything but death parts me from you" (Ruth 1:16-17). In light of the larger Old Testament story, Ruth's decision is monumental: She is turning her back on the gods she grew up with and is fully committing to Naomi's people and her God. *She will be ingrafted as a YHWH-worshiping Israelite.*

I have a friend who became a Christian in response to a sermon by a brash, irreverent preacher who had suspect theology. Years later, when my friend crossed paths with this preacher again, his impression was quite different. After years of spiritual maturing in a healthy church, he told me that he couldn't believe God used a man like that to lead him to the Lord. My friend recognized that this preacher was actually a bad witness but that God had used him *despite* his shortcomings. My friend's experience was a bit like Ruth's: Her ingrafting happened despite Naomi's lack of firm commitment to YHWH. In fact, throughout this scene, Naomi's character is like a dark velvet background that makes the diamond of Ruth's conversion shine.

Ruth's redeemer. When she arrives at her new home, Ruth immediately turns her attention to providing food for her elderly mother-in-law. An earlier Old Testament passage explains her approach: "And when you reap the harvest of your land, you shall not reap your field right up to its edge, nor shall you gather the gleanings after your harvest. You shall leave them for the poor and for the sojourner: I am the Lord your God" (Lev 23:22). Ruth is industrious, and so she starts to glean barley the reapers left behind.

Through more than two decades of marriage, my wife and I have experienced many "coincidences" that turned out to be God's gracious work of providence behind the scenes. Something similar unfolds in Ruth 2. The chapter begins by giving the readers information that Ruth does not yet have: Her dead father-in-law has a relative named Boaz who is a worthy man (Ruth 2:1). Naomi does not have any sons who can marry Ruth, but can one of her husband's other relatives fill this role? As she gleans, Ruth "*happened* to come to the part of the field belonging to Boaz" (Ruth 2:3, emphasis added). What seems like a coincidence will turn out to be a wonderful, providential provision from YHWH. Boaz enters the scene, asks his young employees about the woman he doesn't recognize, and learns she is "the young Moabite woman, who came back with Naomi from the country of Moab" (Ruth 2:6).

Boaz approaches Ruth, tells her how to be least vulnerable as she gleans, gives his young male employees instructions not to touch her, and gives her access to the water reserved for his employees. Ruth cannot believe that she, as a foreigner, would receive such kind treatment, but Boaz is clear:

> All that you have done for your mother-in-law since the death of your husband has been fully told to me, and how you left your father and mother and your native land and came to a people that you did not know before. The LORD repay you for what you have done, and a full reward be given you by the LORD, the God of Israel, under whose wings you have come to take refuge! (Ruth 2:11-12)

Ruth's reputation, along with her conversion, preceded her. She is then allowed to eat Boaz's lunch provisions prepared for his employees. Then, after lunch, Boaz tells his employees to leave extra barley behind for her: She will have abundance from this day of work.

That night, Ruth arrives home with an ephah (about a bushel) of barley and feeds her mother-in-law. Naomi eats and then asks where she gleaned. When she hears Boaz's name, she gives YHWH credit for his kindness. Bitter Naomi now revels in YHWH, "whose kindness has not forsaken the living or the dead!" (Ruth 2:20). So Ruth continues this practice of gleaning in Boaz's fields until the end of the barley and wheat harvests (Ruth 2:23).

Ruth's engagement. At the end of this long season of daily gleaning, Naomi comes up with a plan to help Ruth become Boaz's wife: Ruth will get cleaned up and dressed and then hide on the threshing floor where Boaz will be working. After he finishes eating and drinking, she is to uncover his feet and follow his instructions (Ruth 3:1-5). Ruth follows the plan, and at midnight he is startled to wake up and find a woman at his feet. In the darkness he asks who she is, and Ruth reveals her name and then makes a bold request: "Spread your wings over your servant, for you are a redeemer" (Ruth 3:9). Marion Ann Taylor explains that in that time and place, this was "a symbolic way of saying, 'Marry me!'"[5] Daniel I. Block adds, "As a Moabite, a servant,

[5]Marion Ann Taylor, *Ruth, Esther*, Story of God Bible Commentary (Zondervan Academic, 2020), 60.

and a woman, she could not say so directly, so she expressed her demand metaphorically."[6]

Boaz blesses her by YHWH for not going after a younger man. Instead, she has followed Moses' instructions and asked her dead husband's relative to redeem her by marrying her (see Deut 25:5-6). Boaz then reveals that everyone in Bethlehem recognizes she is a worthy woman (Ruth 3:11). Although this title may not sound very flattering in English, the Hebrew word for "worthy woman" is used in only one other Old Testament book: Proverbs. This is the term used for the excellent wife in Proverbs 31:10.[7] While the book of Proverbs *describes* the ultimate wife that Israelite young men should marry, the book of Ruth *shows her* in story form. In Proverbs we learn about her, and in Ruth we see her in action. Ruth the Moabite has been elevated to the ultimate example of the best kind of wife. As Chris A. Miller and Jason S. DeRouchie put it, "Ruth did not play the part of the foreign temptress who seduced the Israelite Boaz from his calling. Rather, Ruth was a 'worthy woman' who inspired this Bethlehemite to follow the covenant and who, in the end, brought him honor at the city gate."[8]

On cue, the book's plot takes another turn: Although Boaz wants to marry Ruth, there is a nearer relative who has the first right of refusal (Ruth 3:12). If he will not redeem Ruth, Boaz will step in (Ruth 3:13). Before light, Ruth rises to leave, and Boaz sends her away with a large supply of barley (Ruth 3:15). So she returns home and shares what happened with Naomi (Ruth 3:16-18). Although our English Bibles tend to translate Naomi's question along the lines of "How did you fare, my daughter?" (Ruth 3:16), her words in Hebrew are simply, "Who are you, my daughter?" This insight reveals that

[6]Daniel I. Block, *Ruth: A Discourse Analysis of the Hebrew Bible*, Zondervan Exegetical Commentary on the Old Testament (Zondervan Academic, 2015), 180.

[7]This title also occurs in Prov 12:4.

[8]Chris A. Miller and Jason S. DeRouchie, "Ruth," in *What the Old Testament Authors Really Cared About: A Survey of Jesus' Bible*, ed. Jason S. DeRouchie (Kregel Academic, 2013), 329.

Naomi is asking a lot more than simply, "How did it go?" In the words of Waltke, "With this question, Naomi wants to know how Ruth sees herself. Does she identify herself as a scorned woman, a slave girl, or a wife?"[9]

Ruth's redemption. Boaz goes to the gate of the city—the place where visitors enter and also where the town elders oversee business transactions. The other man passes by, and Boaz calls him over. While our English translations usually gloss over his words, Boaz literally says, "Hey, Mr. So-and-So, sit here," or "Hey, Joe Blow, sit here" (Ruth 4:1).[10] The closer relative is not even named by Boaz, much less the story's narrator. As readers, we are meant to feel distance from this man, and we are also meant to be rooting for Boaz.

Boaz gathers ten of the city's elders and resumes the conversation (Ruth 4:2). He explains that Naomi is selling a field and this man wants to purchase it (Ruth 4:3-4). But when Boaz explains that marrying Ruth would be included in the deal, the man declines (Ruth 4:5-6). So in the presence of the city's elders, Boaz strikes a legal agreement with Mr. So-and-So: Boaz will redeem Naomi's field and marry Ruth (Ruth 4:7-10).[11] All the people at the city's gate bless Ruth: May she be like Rachel and Leah, "who together built up the house of Israel" (Ruth 4:11), and may she be "like the house of Perez, whom Tamar bore to Judah" (Ruth 4:12). Ruth is fully committed to YHWH (Ruth 1:16-17), and she has acted so nobly that Boaz and the rest of Bethlehem have recognized her as the ultimate

---

[9]Bruce K. Waltke and Charles Yu, *An Old Testament Theology: An Exegetical, Canonical, and Thematic Approach* (Zondervan, 2007), 858.

[10]See Waltke and Yu, *Old Testament Theology*, 859.

[11]Hill and Walton explain, "An expanded interpretation of this custom of levirate marriage is combined with land redemption rights to provide the legal setting for the book of Ruth. The Hebrew term *gōʾēl* (kinsman-redeemer) is taken from the land redemption law (Lev. 25:25-31, 47-55). According to this law, land sold by a person could be bought back by a relative so as to keep the land in the family." Andrew E. Hill and John H. Walton, *A Survey of the Old Testament*, 4th ed. (Zondervan Academic, 2023), 175.

example of the ideal wife (Ruth 3:11). In this scene the townsfolk liken her to the most prominent *Israelite* women in the Old Testament. Waltke adds,

> Both Naomi and Boaz call Ruth "my daughter," identifying the natural-born Moabitess as a true daughter in Israel (Ruth 2:8; 3:1). The community recognizes her as better than seven sons (4:15). Her speeches show she is obedient to the older generation of the family into which she married (2:8-9; 2:22-23; 3:1-6, 12-15). But her first allegiance is to God (*I AM*) and to Israel, not to family (1:16).[12]

YHWH gives her conception, and she bears a son (Ruth 4:13). The women of the city bless YHWH for his provision of a redeemer and name the baby Obed, saying, "A son has been born to Naomi" (Ruth 4:17). In light of Moses' instructions in Deuteronomy, this first son is Naomi's heir. We learn next that Obed will father Jesse, who will father David. As a joyfully shocking ending, we discover that Ruth will be the great-grandmother of the greatest king in the history of Israel.

Ruth's genealogy. The book of Ruth doesn't end there. It continues with five final verses of genealogy. These verses begin with Perez, the son of Judah, and just like the book of Genesis, the lineage of redemption is traced.[13] As we remember Jacob's blessing that "the scepter shall not depart from Judah" (Gen 49:10), this genealogy from Judah's son, Perez, through Boaz, Obed, and Jesse to David, is striking. Not only is Ruth ingrafted into Israel, but she also becomes a lived-out example of the ideal wife (Ruth 3:11; cf. Prov 31:10) as well as the great-grandmother of Israel's greatest king, David (Ruth 4:18-22). Waltke adds, "In this genealogy Boaz fills the favored seventh slot, and David, the tenth slot of completion, just as in Genesis 5

---

[12]Waltke and Yu, *Old Testament Theology*, 864-65.

[13]For a more thorough explanation of genealogies in the Bible, see the chapter "Genealogy: The Lineage of Redemption," in Ian J. Vaillancourt, *The Dawning of Redemption: The Story of the Pentateuch and the Hope of the Gospel* (Crossway, 2022), 71-88.

Enoch and Noah respectively fill these slots."[14] Just as the genealogies in Genesis trace the lineage of redemption, the surprise ending of Ruth does the same through a woman who was born an idolatrous Moabite. And her full *ingrafting* is a wonderful foretaste of YHWH's blessing of all the families of the earth through the descendants of Abraham (Gen 12:3).

INGRAFTING AND THE WRITINGS

As though these blessings from the little book of Ruth could not be contained, its placement in the Hebrew Old Testament also spills over into blessing in other books.

In our English Bibles, Ruth follows Judges: Joshua, Judges, *Ruth*. Why? We find the answer in the first line of the book: "In the days when the judges ruled" (Ruth 1:1). According to the logic that led to this placement, the book of Ruth should come after Judges because these books are in the same genre. They are stories. And according to this logic, Ruth should also come after Judges because of chronology. The events in Ruth took place "when the judges ruled."

As we scan table I.1, concerning the earliest attested Hebrew order for the Old Testament, we find Ruth in a completely different place. According to this Hebrew order, Ruth comes *before Psalms*, as the first book in the Writings—the third section of the Hebrew Old Testament. This is explained by theme. According to their titles, David wrote at least 73 out of 150 psalms. In fact, the book of Psalms was often referred to as "David" by Jews of this period. Why would Ruth come immediately before the Psalms in this order of books? Because of the way it ends, with the genealogy of Ruth and Boaz's son, Obed. According to this way of thinking, the book of Ruth acts as a preface to the Psalms. It leads us to David.

---

[14]Waltke and Yu, *Old Testament Theology*, 861.

Even beyond the genealogy, Stephen G. Dempster points out that by the time a reader of the Old Testament in its Hebrew order encounters Ruth and Psalms, they have read of David's origin in Bethlehem (1 Sam 16), YHWH's covenant promise that a son of David will reign on his throne forever (2 Sam 7), and of a coming royal Messiah who will be from Bethlehem and will be great to the ends of the earth (Mic 5:2-4).[15] In the book of Ruth, we learn of David's hometown of Bethlehem and of the Gentile (non-Jewish) person in his lineage—Ruth. With the book of Ruth as its preface, Dempster argues that the book of Psalms is read through the lens of the "messianic birth narrative" in Ruth, and so it highlights messianic hope in a savior who will be for all peoples—Jews and non-Jews. This reinforces that the order of Old Testament books affects the way we hear the story.

When Ruth is read in its placement in the earliest attested Hebrew Old Testament order, we learn that David's Moabite great-grandma embodied the lesson that the people of God would be bigger than one nation. Ruth's ingrafting signals to us the beginning of something much bigger and better, something that the coming Messiah (who is attested in the Psalms and throughout the Writings) will usher in. Dempster puts it well once again:

> But this does not just have implications for the Davidic dynasty; the story shows that the Davidic dynasty has implications for the nations. When Ruth first meets Boaz, he praises her for finding refuge under the "wings" of Yahweh (. . . Ruth 2:12). When she reminds him of his responsibility as a kinsman redeemer, she tells him to spread the "wing" (. . . 3:9) of his garment over her. His marriage to her anticipates the nations' finding refuge under the wings of Yahweh through a Davidic descendant.[16]

[15]See Stephen G. Dempster, "A Wandering Moabite: Ruth—A Book in Search of a Canonical Home," in *The Shape of the Writings*, ed. Julius Steinberg and Timothy J. Stone, Siphrut 16 (Eisenbrauns, 2015), 100.

[16]Stephen G. Dempster, *Dominion and Dynasty: A Theology of the Hebrew Bible*, New Studies in Biblical Theology 15 (InterVarsity Press, 2003), 194.

This is on full display near the end of the Writings, in 2 Chronicles 6:32-33. Included in Solomon's prayer of dedication for the temple is this promise:

> Likewise, when a foreigner, who is not of your people Israel, comes from a far country for the sake of your great name and your mighty hand and your outstretched arm, when he comes and prays toward this house, hear from heaven your dwelling place and do according to all for which the foreigner calls to you, in order that all the peoples of the earth may know your name and fear you, as do your people Israel, and that they may know that this house that I have built is called by your name. (2 Chron 6:32-33)

LOOKING FORWARD TO CHRIST: NON-JEWISH CHRISTIANS ARE INGRAFTED OLIVE SHOOTS

As we turn to the New Testament, we shouldn't be surprised that it begins with a genealogy. Matthew's purpose is to link Jesus back to David and Abraham. Tracing Jesus' lineage back to Abraham calls to mind the promise that in him (and his descendants), all the families of the earth would be blessed (Gen 12:3; 18:18; 22:18; cf. Gen 28:14). As this lineage is traced, four women are named, and this was not usual practice in the ancient world. These include the Canaanite Tamar, who bore Perez to Judah; the Canaanite Rahab, who bore Boaz to Salmon; the Moabite Ruth; who married Boaz and was the great-grandmother of King David; and Bathsheba, who was the wife of a Hittite named Uriah before she married David and gave birth to Solomon (Mt 1:1-17). Not only were these women *ingrafted* into God's people, but they were also *elevated* above Israelite women as matriarchs in the line of Jesus, the Messiah.

How does this ingrafting theme apply to Christians? Paul tells us in Ephesians that Gentiles (another name for non-Jews) were once "separated from Christ, alienated from the commonwealth of Israel and strangers to the covenants of promise, having no hope and without God in the world" (Eph 2:12). But in Christ, Christian Gentiles "have been brought near by the blood of Christ" (Eph 2:13). Jesus broke down the dividing wall of hostility between Jews and non-Jews and made peace (Eph 2:14). Since Jesus fulfilled the Old Testament hope, a person's new primary orientation would not be national.

My pastor-friend likes to tell married couples that their primary relational identity used to be as son or daughter of their parents. Although they continue to be a son or daughter who is called to honor their parents after they are married, their new primary relational identity is now as husband or wife of their spouse. In a similar way, the Old Testament tells the story of initial fulfillments of all the families of the earth being blessed through Abraham and his descendants. Rahab and Ruth are two examples. In the coming of Christ, this has been fully realized, such that being "in Christ" is now a person's primary identity marker. The Christian church is a beautifully multiethnic fellowship of God's redeemed people, such as Rahab, Ruth, you, and me.

In another place, the apostle Paul likens this phenomenon of non-Jews as full members of God's people to a mass ingrafting:

> But if some of the branches were broken off, and you, although a wild olive shoot, were grafted in among the others and now share in the nourishing root of the olive tree, do not be arrogant toward the branches. If you are, remember it is not you who support the root, but the root that supports you. Then you will say, "Branches were broken off so that I might be grafted in." That is true. They were broken off because of their unbelief, but you stand fast through faith. So do not become proud, but fear. For if God did not spare the natural branches, neither will he spare you. Note then the kindness and the severity of God: severity toward those who have fallen, but God's kindness to you, provided you continue in his kindness. Otherwise you too will be cut off. And even they, if they do not continue in their unbelief, will be grafted in, for God has the power to graft them in again. For

> if you were cut from what is by nature a wild olive tree, and grafted, contrary to nature, into a cultivated olive tree, how much more will these, the natural branches, be grafted back into their own olive tree. (Rom 11:17-24)

Paul is saying that a vast number of ethnic Jews will one day turn to Christ as their Savior and Lord. Until then, a vast number of non-Jewish wild olive shoots are being grafted into Christ.

This all leads to a beautifully multiethnic song in heaven, where the four living creatures and the twenty-four elders celebrate Jesus: "For you were slain, and by your blood you ransomed people for God *from every tribe and language and people and nation*" (Rev 5:9, emphasis added; cf. Rev 14:6). There will be no sun or moon in the new Jerusalem, "for the glory of God gives it light, and its lamp is the Lamb" (Rev 21:23). By this light "will *the nations* walk, and *the kings of the earth* will bring their glory into it" (Rev 21:24, emphasis added). In this place, the leaves of the tree of life will be "for the healing of *the nations*" (Rev 22:2, emphasis added). As those who have been grafted into Christ, Christians look forward with a certain hope to the day when they will join the ultimate multiethnic chorus for eternity.

DISCUSSION QUESTIONS

1. Explain the horticultural practice of grafting a shoot into the trunk of a healthier tree.
2. Prior to reading this chapter, had you ever noticed the way the theme of ingrafting can be traced from Genesis to Revelation?
3. Share some Old Testament examples of non-Jews who were grafted into Israel (other than Ruth). Hint: For another example, read 2 Kings 5. Another hint: Read the book of Jonah.
4. Share some new things this chapter taught you about the book of Ruth.

5. How does the placement of Ruth in the earliest attested Hebrew Old Testament order affect our reading of the Psalms and the entire Writings section? Share specific examples.
6. Read Psalms 47:9; 117:1-2 as a group. How has this chapter shed light on these verses?
7. Was the multiethnic Christian church plan B in God's unfolding story of redemption, or does understanding the theme of ingrafting in the Old Testament lead us to a different conclusion?

SOJOURN

PRESERVING THE REDEEMED

THEIR PARENTS AND GRANDPARENTS had been stolen away, but for the people in our story, their family's place of sojourn was home. In an earlier chapter we witnessed the devastation of Judah's defeat by the Babylonians and their exile to Babylon. In this chapter we will reflect on those who obeyed YHWH's command to settle into their foreign residence and to seek the welfare of their new (temporary) home (Jer 29:4-7).

The books of Daniel and Esther are both records of YHWH preserving his redeemed people of Israel during their sojourn. The earliest attested Hebrew order of Old Testament books tells Israel's story of sojourn while Babylon was the world superpower (Daniel) and later, when Persia was the strongest nation in the world (Esther), before it recounts the initial return from exile (Ezra–Nehemiah), and the ultimate hope of full restoration (Chronicles).

Though in this chapter we'll focus on Esther, we should at least note a few details from Daniel. The story of Daniel and his friends took place when the sting of exile was still fresh, just after King Nebuchadnezzar of Babylon had defeated Judah, destroyed the temple, and carried away its wealth and its leading citizens into exile in 587/586 BC. Between Daniel and Esther, Cyrus the Great conquered Babylon in 539 BC.

In our next chapter we will learn about Cyrus's proclamation that allowed the Jews to return to Jerusalem and rebuild the temple and city. We'll witness three waves of return over the course of about one hundred years under the leadership of four successive Persian kings: Cyrus, Darius, Ahasuerus, and Artaxerxes (see Ezra 4:4-7). The events in the book of Esther took place under the third Persian king, Ahasuerus, who reigned from 485–465 BC.[1] These events happened after the first returnees left Persia for Jerusalem in 538 BC but before the returns under Ezra (458 BC) and Nehemiah (444 BC). This means that Esther and her family had chosen to stay in Persia, at least for the time being.[2] The remainder of this chapter will focus on her story.[3]

THE STORY OF ESTHER: YHWH PRESERVES HIS SOJOURNING REDEEMED

The story of Esther begins and ends with two banquets.[4] The two banquets at the beginning of the story take place in "the royal city of Susa, at the heart of the vast Persian empire" (located in modern Iran).[5] Readers of Esther are not told the occasion for these feasts, but we do get a peek into the indulgence of the king. According to historical records, King Ahasuerus had just led an unsuccessful invasion of Greece and entered a period of sensual overindulgence.[6] This explains the extended feasts at the beginning of the book.

---

[1]See Bruce K. Waltke and Charles Yu, *An Old Testament Theology: An Exegetical, Canonical, and Thematic Approach* (Zondervan, 2007), 765.

[2]See Gary V. Smith, "Esther," in *What the Old Testament Authors Really Cared About: A Survey of Jesus' Bible*, ed. Jason S. DeRouchie (Kregel Academic, 2013), 420.

[3]This is partly due to the space restrictions of the chapter and the overlap in the general theme of sojourn through these two books. Daniel is also half story and half apocalyptic literature, and in order to do the book justice, more space would be needed than this chapter allows.

[4]I first gleaned this insight from Andreas J. Köstenberger and Gregory Goswell, *Biblical Theology: A Canonical, Thematic, and Ethical Approach* (Crossway, 2023), 311.

[5]Barry G. Webb, *Five Festal Garments: Christian Reflections on the Song of Songs, Ruth, Lamentations, Ecclesiastes, and Esther*, New Studies in Biblical Theology 10 (InterVarsity Press, 2000), 117; see also Karen H. Jobes, *Esther*, New International Version Application Commentary (Zondervan Academic, 1999), 28.

[6]See Jobes, *Esther*, 28, 94.

King Ahasuerus is cast in the story as a royal buffoon, one who is publicly thwarted by his wife when he tries to show off her beauty to his guests. David Firth humorously explains that "anyone with an irony-deficiency needs to have it addressed before they proceed further. The king claims great power, but will turn out to be powerless in the matter of convincing his wife to come to the party."[7] In other words, this book is meant to make us chuckle.

The bumbling king is not sure how to respond to this humiliation, so he consults advisers. They worry that other women in the empire might follow Queen Vashti's example if something is not done. So Vashti is banished from the king's presence permanently, and a search begins for her replacement (Esther 1:19-22).

After a while, the royal attendants gather beautiful virgins to the harem in Susa, where they will go through a twelve-month regimen of oil, myrrh, spices, and ointments for more beautification (Esther 2:1-4, 12). This sets the stage for the introduction of Mordecai the Jew and his relative Hadassah (also called Esther), whom he has raised since her parents' deaths. Karen Jobes notes, "The name *Marduka* means 'man' or 'worshiper' of Marduk, the male deity of the Babylonians."[8] This is a reminder that not only was this faithful Jew sojourning away from the land YHWH had promised to his people, but he also has been given a new name in order to be incorporated into those people. This is likely also the case with Hadassah (a Hebrew name that means "myrtle"), who has been given the Persian name Esther (which may also mean "myrtle") as a constant reminder of her sojourn in Persia.[9] No doubt being taken into the harem of an uncircumcised, indulgent Persian king would also have been a reminder that Esther was sojourning far from the land of her people.

---

[7]David G. Firth, *The Message of Esther*, The Bible Speaks Today (IVP Academic, 2010), 37. For similar sentiments, see Webb, *Five Festal Garments*, 125.

[8]Jobes, *Esther*, 96.

[9]E. A. Phillips, "Esther 6: Person," in *Dictionary of the Old Testament: Wisdom, Poetry and Writings*, ed. Tremper Longman III and Peter Enns (InterVarsity Press, 2008), 188.

When the twelve months of beautification are complete, the king begins to summon one woman each night—when he will take each one's virginity and decide who will become his new queen (Esther 2:12-14). Esther is summoned, and we learn that "the king loved Esther more than all the women, and she won grace and favor in his sight more than all the virgins, so that he set the royal crown on her head and made her queen instead of Vashti" (Esther 2:17).

The book of Esther exhibits many tensions between YHWH's instructions for how his redeemed people are to live and how Mordecai and Esther behave. For example, in the Torah YHWH instructs his people, "You shall not intermarry with [non-Jews], giving your daughters to their sons or taking their daughters for your sons, for they would turn away your sons from following me, to serve other gods. Then the anger of the LORD would be kindled against you, and he would destroy you quickly" (Deut 7:3-4). In Esther, Mordecai witnesses his orphaned relative being taken away to have sex outside marriage and then marrying an idolatrous foreign king. She also feasts with him, "in apparent disregard of Jewish dietary laws."[10]

Nevertheless, with Esther as queen the stage is set for the plot of the book. In Esther 2:19 we encounter Mordecai sitting at the king's gate. Although Western readers may assume that this is incidental information, something more is being revealed: "That Mordecai was sitting at the king's gate apparently means that he was a high-ranking government official. It was at the city gate where important business was transacted."[11] Because of this position, Mordecai discovers a plot against the king's life. Since Esther is now the queen, this information can be swiftly communicated, and the plot is thwarted.

All of this sets the story up for its main conflict, between "the Jews" (so designated in the book forty times and represented by "Mordecai the Jew"; Esther 6:10; 8:7; 9:29, 31; 10:3; cf. Esther 5:13), and Haman,

---

[10]Webb, *Five Festal Garments*, 120.

[11]W. Hall Harris, ed., *The NET Bible Notes* (Biblical Studies Press, 2005), Esther 2:19, n36.

"the enemy of the Jews" (Esther 3:10; 8:1; 9:10, 24; cf. Esther 7:6).[12] While the book began with two *Persian* feasts that set the scene for its main plot, it concludes with two *Jewish* feasts—Purim—which are initiated to celebrate the story's great reversal. In the end, Mordecai is elevated in the kingdom, Haman is hanged on the gallows he constructed for Mordecai, the Jewish people are preserved from genocide, and a new annual feast is initiated as a reminder that YHWH preserved his redeemed during their sojourn. As Köstenberger and Goswell put it, "The main themes of the book of Esther are the threat to the existence of the Jews, and the indestructability of God's people."[13] Most surprising of all, the book of Esther manages to communicate all of these things without mentioning God even once.

READING ESTHER IN LIGHT OF THE CANON

If new readers of the Bible were to encounter the book of Esther *first*, before reading other parts, the story would certainly be riveting.[14] If experienced apart from the rest of the Old Testament story, readers would quickly gain a sense that the Jews are the good guys and that through many trials they will endure and even be strengthened. But when we read the book of Esther through the lens of the broader Old Testament story, the book's theology—its teaching about God and how he relates to his people—comes into sharp focus. Why? Because this book, which doesn't mention the name of God, is filled with links to the rest of the Old Testament teaching about who God is and how he deals with his people. Firth explains: "It is by pointing readers to the wider record of Scripture that the book of Esther is able to highlight its own theology. . . . Such reflection offers insights not available to those outside, who can only see that something is happening, whilst

[12]See Webb, *Five Festal Garments*, 116-17.

[13]Köstenberger and Goswell, *Biblical Theology*, 311.

[14]For a book-length (and thus more in-depth) exploration of Esther in light of the canon, see David G. Firth and Brittany N. Melton, eds., *Reading Esther Intertextually*, The Library of Hebrew Bible/Old Testament Studies 725 (T&T Clark, 2022).

also providing us with a framework for understanding our experience more clearly."[15] The more we fill our minds with the entire Old Testament story, therefore, the more the book of Esther will come alive.

Let's look at a few examples. First, Paul House notices that the preservation of the Jews in Esther complements the same theme in the story of Joseph (Gen 37–50), in the exodus from Egypt (Ex 1–18), and in the conquest of the Promised Land (Josh 6–12).[16] To this we could add the preservation of Daniel and his friends. This means that we should read Esther as another example of YHWH's care for his people, even though the book of Esther never mentions him.

Getting more specific, when Esther decides to carry out Mordecai's plan to enter the presence of the king to plead for the life of the Jews, she calls a three-day fast among the Jews. For readers who are unfamiliar with the rest of the biblical story, the mention of a fast would likely hint toward a posture of grief, earnestness and desperation, and solidarity among all who would participate. But what does the rest of the Old Testament teach about fasting? Whether implied or explicitly stated, fasting in the Old Testament is often linked to earnest *prayer*.[17] For example, Ezra reports that those who are returning to Jerusalem "proclaimed a fast . . . at the river Ahava, that we might humble ourselves before our God, to seek from him a safe journey for ourselves, our children, and all our goods. . . . We fasted and implored our God for this, and he listened to our entreaty" (Ezra 8:21, 23). According to this passage, fasting brought a posture of humility before God as the people sought earnestly for a safe journey. Once again, as we read the book of Esther in light of the rest of the Old Testament canon, our understanding of the story is significantly deepened: Earnest prayer is implied in this scene.

---

[15]Firth, *Message of Esther*, 123.

[16]See Paul R. House, *Old Testament Theology* (InterVarsity Press, 1998), 492.

[17]Fasting in the Old Testament is also linked to mourning and repentance. For mourning, see, e.g., 1 Sam 31:13; 2 Sam 1:12. For repentance, see, e.g., Ezra 9:5; Neh 9:1; Dan 9:3.

Let's look at just one more example of reading Esther in light of the canon. The conflict between Mordecai and Haman offers drama to anyone who loves a gripping story of unjust persecution and an unlikely reversal. In the story, Mordecai is presented as a victim—his nation lost in war, and his house and security were taken as he was forced to live in a foreign land. Mordecai is also presented as noble and upright, as he has raised his younger relative because she has no parents—presumably because they were killed in the battle with Babylon. However, when we read the book of Esther in light of the canon, the theme of YHWH preserving the redeemed in exile is brought into vivid focus.

A first hint comes in the initial description of Mordecai: He is a Jew, "the son of Jair, son of Shimei, son of Kish, a Benjaminite" (Esther 2:5). Readers of Samuel will remember that King Saul was the son of Kish, and he was from the tribe of Benjamin (1 Sam 9:1-2). Another hint comes in the initial description of Mordecai's chief rival: "Haman the Agagite" (Esther 3:1). Readers of Samuel may also remember that Agag was the king of the Amalekites, who were enemies of Israel (1 Sam 15:8). So the conflict in the book of Esther is actually between a descendant of Kish, the Benjaminite (and therefore also a descendant of King Saul), and a descendant of King Agag, the Amalekite.

What does the rest of the Old Testament story teach about these people groups? In Exodus 17 we learn that "Amalek came and fought with Israel at Rephidim" (Ex 17:8). This was in the context of the exodus from Egypt, and Amalak attacked a weary people (Deut 25:17-18). After YHWH granted Israel the victory, he made a promise: "Write this as a memorial in a book and recite it in the ears of Joshua, that I will utterly blot out the memory of Amalek from under heaven" (Ex 17:14). As part of his response, Moses acknowledged, "The LORD will have war with Amalek from generation to generation" (Ex 17:16). Although Amalek and his descendants would one day be totally annihilated (Ex 17:14), YHWH would have war with this people group for a long time—from generation to generation—before this would be fully accomplished (Ex 17:16). However, once Israel reached the land, they were given the command by YHWH: "You shall blot out the memory of Amalek from under heaven; you shall not forget" (Deut 25:19).

This leads us to 1 Samuel 15, where YHWH's anointed king, Saul, was told by YHWH's prophet Samuel: "Thus says the Lord of hosts, 'I have noted what Amalek did to Israel in opposing them on the way when they came up out of Egypt. Now go and strike Amalek and devote to destruction all that they have. Do not spare them, but kill both man and woman, child and infant, ox and sheep, camel and donkey'" (1 Sam 15:2-3).

This battle took place more than five hundred years after YHWH's promise in Exodus 17 and his command to Israel in Deuteronomy 25. Clearly, nothing had changed, because through his prophet, YHWH gave Saul a clear command to devote this enemy people to destruction. In the battle that ensued, things looked very promising, because "Saul defeated the Amalekites from Havilah as far as Shur, which is east of Egypt" (1 Sam 15:7). However, trouble followed:

> And [Saul] took Agag the king of the Amalekites alive and devoted to destruction all the people with the edge of the sword. But Saul and the people spared Agag and the best of the sheep and of the oxen and of the fattened calves and the lambs, and all that was good, and would not utterly destroy them. All that was despised and worthless they devoted to destruction. (1 Sam 15:8-9)

This clear disobedience led to YHWH's rejection of Saul as king (1 Sam 15:11, 23, 26). In this scene, the son of Kish, a Benjaminite, failed to carry out YHWH's command to put the Amalekite king, Agag, to death.

Does this sound familiar? Although Samuel the prophet obeyed where Saul had failed, putting Agag to death by the sword (1 Sam 15:33), evidently he had surviving descendants. We know this because the plot of Esther is framed around a descendant of Kish named Mordecai obeying where Saul had failed by gaining victory over a descendant of Agag named Haman. This means that the death of Haman at the end of Esther is not merely to be read as an inspiring story of reversal, in which the aggressor is destroyed by the one he so ruthlessly and unjustly tried to kill. When we read Esther in light of the canon, we discover that its message of the preservation of the Jewish people comes in direct fulfillment of YHWH's previous promises to his redeemed people.[18] All of a sudden, a book that doesn't even mention the name of God is filled with teaching about God's amazing faithfulness and his absolute commitment to preserve his precious people.

Before we spend time looking forward to Christ, we need to ask why. Why does the book of Esther present its theology so subtly—with no mention of God at all? In many ways, the book of Esther offers rich teaching about God's sovereignty and faithfulness. But it accomplishes this teaching *subtly*, by intentionally calling to mind links with other parts of Scripture.

A clue may be found in its first setting and its first readers: Since the book of Esther tells the story of YHWH preserving his redeemed in exile without telling of their exit out of Persia and return to Israel, we can infer that its first readers would have been Jews living in Persian exile *as well as the Persians themselves*. The links to the rest of the Old Testament would have allowed the Jews—who would have been familiar with Scripture—to read the book and make the same connections we have noticed. But the subtlety of the book's teaching also meant that it would not have been received as threatening by

[18]Dempster adds, "Just as there is a significant echo of Baalam's prophecies in Daniel, so this is continued in Esther: 'their king shall be higher than Agag, their kingdom shall be exalted' (Num. 24:7), and 'Amalek is doomed to perish for ever' (Num. 24:20)." Stephen G. Dempster, *Dominion and Dynasty: A Theology of the Hebrew Bible*, New Studies in Biblical Theology 15 (InterVarsity Press, 2003), 222.

readers from Persia. This would have been especially true if the book was written after the death of King Ahasuerus—something suggested by the backward gaze of Esther 1:1.[19] Although the book of Esther presents him as an inept king, it is likely that the Persians themselves would have agreed with this portrait. So this presentation would not have been likely to offend the later Persian readers—especially since the book as a whole is pro-Persia. The book of Esther is subversive: It screams its deeply theological message to those whose minds are filled with the Word of God, and it hides this same message from those who would be offended by it.

LOOKING FORWARD TO CHRIST: RAISED ON THE THIRD DAY ACCORDING TO THE SCRIPTURES

Near the end of his first letter to the Corinthian church, the apostle Paul summarizes what he deems to be "of first importance": "that Christ died for our sins in accordance with the Scriptures, that he was buried, that he was raised on the third day in accordance with the Scriptures, and that he appeared to [numerous people whom Paul names in 1 Cor 15:5-8]" (1 Cor 15:3-5).

In this passage, we find four key words about Christ: He *died*, was *buried*, was *raised*, and *appeared*. This is the gospel in a nutshell—and a great sermon or Bible study outline! It is absolutely core to the gospel that Jesus *died* for our sins, that he was *buried*, that he was *raised* on the third day, and that he *appeared* to numerous individuals and groups. As we look closely at this passage, it is also clear that these things were taught in the Old Testament—what Paul calls "the Scriptures." Specifically, Paul says Christ's death for our sins and his resurrection on the third day are "in accordance with the Scriptures" (1 Cor 15:3-4). This is extremely glorious on many levels: Our sins

[19]The following seems to be written from the perspective of one who lived after its events: "Now in the days of Ahasuerus, the Ahasuerus who reigned from India to Ethiopia over 127 provinces, in those days when King Ahasuerus sat on his royal throne in Susa, the citadel" (Esther 1:1-2).

have been paid for by Christ's death. And his death and resurrection were not plan B in the mind of God. No, they were *the plan* all along—these things were taught *in the Old Testament.*

This New Testament passage not only leads us to revel in our standing in Christ; it also compels us to read the Old Testament with a fresh set of lenses. If the apostle Paul's ministry was marked by preaching that Christ died for our sins and was raised on the third day *according to the Old Testament Scriptures*, then we should read the Old Testament and ask, *Where*? Where does the Old Testament teach that Christ would come and die for our sins? And where does the Old Testament teach that Christ would be raised from the dead, particularly *on the third day*?

Initial help for putting this together comes from the lips of Jesus. In response to a request for a sign from the scribes and Pharisees, he says,

> An evil and adulterous generation seeks for a sign, but no sign will be given to it except the sign of the prophet Jonah. For just as Jonah was *three days and three nights* in the belly of the great fish, so will the Son of Man be *three days and three nights* in the heart of the earth. The men of Nineveh will rise up at the judgment with this generation and condemn it, for they repented at the preaching of Jonah, and behold, something greater than Jonah is here. (Mt 12:39-41, emphasis added)

According to Jesus, we are meant to read the book of Jonah and recognize that Jesus is greater than Jonah—he didn't merely live in the belly of a great fish (like Jonah did) but actually died a real death and then was raised from the dead. Also notice that Jesus mentions *three days and three nights* for both Jonah and the Son of Man (see Jon 1:17). Jesus read the Old Testament and was pointed to his coming third-day resurrection.[20] In fact, the people of Nineveh, who repented when the

---

[20]Stephen G. Dempster is helpful on this point: "The ancient Israelite conceptions of death and life should not be viewed in a reductionistic manner as the mere termination of physical existence, a view associated more with notions in modern, western medicine. In my judgment this

"resurrected" Jonah preached to them, will rise up and condemn those who in Jesus' day did not repent when one greater than Jonah came to fulfill the Old Testament hope. And Jesus calls this a sign that will authenticate his entire ministry.

This leads us to ask whether any other Old Testament passages hint at a third-day resurrection for the coming Messiah. Stephen G. Dempster is insightful as he leads us to search for occurrences of the phrase "third day" or "day three" in the Old Testament.[21] Of course, some of the references have nothing to do with a coming resurrection of Jesus on the third day. But a surprising number of these do show someone who was as good as dead and was delivered from death on day three.

For example, Genesis 22 is the powerful account of God testing Abraham by telling him to sacrifice his only son, Isaac, on a mountain. On the journey, Abraham makes a startling claim: He and Isaac will go and worship, and he and Isaac will come back again (Gen 22:5). As readers, we may be tempted to ask whether Abraham was lying to the people in the story. After all, he knew that he was about to sacrifice his son on a mountain. But the author of Hebrews interprets this differently: "By faith Abraham, when he was tested, offered up Isaac, and he who had received the promises was in the act of offering up his only son, of whom it was said, 'Through Isaac shall your offspring be named.' He considered that God was able even to raise him from the dead, from which, figuratively speaking, he did receive him back" (Heb 11:17-19).

---

is the major problem with the predominant view of scholarship which argues that belief in resurrection was an extremely late development in the OT. It constructs the theoretical net of resurrection belief in a certain western way so that it is only able to catch a certain type of 'fish,' and then it concludes that other smaller examples of the same fish that have slipped through its mesh do not exist. The problem of course is with the mesh, not the existence of the fish. . . . The biblical view, however, is far more dynamic." Dempster, "From Slight Peg to Cornerstone to Capstone: The Resurrection of Christ on 'The Third Day' According to the Scriptures," *Westminster Theological Journal* 76, no. 2 (2014): 385.

[21]See Dempster, "From Slight Peg," 371-409.

Since the New Testament is the inspired answer key to the Old Testament, we learn that Abraham made this statement in faith because he believed that Isaac would return with him. Why? Because he believed that God was even able to raise the dead. So when God stopped Abraham from sacrificing his son, the author of Hebrews tells us that Abraham did, figuratively speaking, receive his son back from the dead. Why? Because Isaac was as good as dead. This was a sort of resurrection that pointed to the actual resurrection of the coming Messiah, the one greater than Isaac.

As we look closely at the details of Genesis 22, we see, "*On the third day* Abraham lifted up his eyes and saw the place from afar" (Gen 22:4, emphasis added). In this text Abraham makes a three-day journey to sacrifice his son. For three days, Abraham journeys, knowing what he is going to do. And for three days, Abraham trusts that God can raise the dead. Therefore, according to Genesis 22:4, Abraham received Isaac back *on the third day*.

Although we could look at many other examples of Old Testament pointers to a third-day resurrection of the coming Messiah, Dempster points to one that is particularly relevant for our current chapter: Esther 5:1. In context, Haman has already convinced King Ahasuerus to sign orders "to destroy, to kill, and to annihilate all Jews" (Esther 3:13). In response, Mordecai has gone into mourning and sent word about this plan through one of Esther's attendants. Mordecai then commands Esther "to go to the king to beg us favor and plead with him on behalf of her people" (Esther 4:8). Esther then points out the problem with this plan: "All the king's servants and the people of the king's provinces know that if any man or woman goes to the king inside the inner court without being called, there is but one law—to be put to death, except the one to whom the king holds out the golden scepter so that he may live. But as for me, I have not been called to come in to the king these thirty days" (Esther 4:11).

Through the back-and-forth of messengers, Mordecai hears of the risk this plan will bring to Esther, but he is adamant: "Do not think to yourself that in the king's palace you will escape any more than all the other Jews. For if you keep silent at this time, relief and deliverance will rise for the Jews from another place, but you and your father's house will perish. And who knows whether you have not come to the kingdom for such a time as this?" (Esther 4:13-14). Esther then responds with resolve: She will risk her life by going to the king, but only after all the Jews in Susa fast—with prayer implied—on her behalf *for three days.*

Does this sound familiar? In the moment that Esther decides to follow through with Mordecai's plan, she is choosing death for herself. After a period of three days, she will go to the king. Even though this is against the law of Persia, Esther will do it. She adds, "And if I perish, I perish" (Esther 4:16). She is willing to die for this cause. Esther 5:1 then reveals when Esther went to the king: *on the third day.* As the story unfolds, Queen Esther enters the presence of the king, he holds out the golden scepter, and she touches its tip (Esther 5:2). In that moment—on the third day after she chose sure death for herself in order to save God's people—she is given life again. In the end, the Jews are saved, the wicked Haman is put to death, and Esther receives her life back.

As we take our cues about how to read the Old Testament from the apostle Paul (in 1 Cor 15:4), Jesus (in Mt 12:39-41), and the author of Hebrews (in Heb 11:17-19), we discover that we should be searching the Old Testament for people with as-good-as-dead experiences whose plights were turned around on the third day. God intends these stories to point us to the one who would experience the true and ultimate third-day resurrection, because Jesus died a real death for our sins and then was raised from the dead on the third day (1 Cor 15:3-4). Jobes puts it beautifully:

> This scene [in Esther 5] pictures a gracious act of a king who holds life-and-death power. Had God not extended the cross of Jesus Christ to the world, all would die in his presence. "On the third day" after the final judgment transpired on the cross, Jesus Christ arose to imperishable life, guaranteeing safety to enter God's presence to all who reach out in faith to touch that cross-shaped sceptre.[22]

All of a sudden, Esther's resolve is not *merely* an example for us to follow. It also gives us a powerful Old Testament picture of chosen death and deliverance from death on the third day that prepares us to understand, accept, and revel in the work of Jesus for us.

DISCUSSION QUESTIONS

1. What are some specific examples of irony in the way Esther 1 paints King Ahasuerus?
2. How does this book present Mordecai and Esther as examples of God granting favor and using undeserving people to accomplish his ultimate purposes?
3. How is Esther's fast intended to call to mind other parts of the Old Testament that fill out the book with the theology of the Old Testament for its Jewish readers?
4. How do the respective lineages of both Mordecai and Haman place the book of Esther in the flow of the overall Old Testament story?
5. In this chapter we noticed several examples of third-day resurrections in the Old Testament. Can you think of any more? Would it help if you looked up the words *three* and *third* in a concordance? Do you agree that these are meant to prepare our minds for the third-day resurrection of Jesus? Hint: Read, for example, 2 Samuel 24; 2 Kings 20:5-6; Hosea 6:1-3.

---

[22]Jobes, *Esther*, 147.

8

RETURN AND REBUILDING

A SECOND REDEMPTION (PARTLY) ACCOMPLISHED

My wife and I were planning the trip of a lifetime. After lots of research, we booked a campsite along a picturesque 298-kilometer (185-mile) trail on Canada's east coast. But after days in the car, we finally arrived and were *horrified*: Our campsite was noisy, and our view was horrible. After a restless night, we found a marginally better campsite the next day, and on that trail we encountered whales on a boat tour, moose on the road, and breathtaking scenery. Although we made wonderful memories on our trip, it didn't fully live up to our expectations. Something similar is true of the next book(s) in our study.

While Ezra and Nehemiah are presented as two books in most English Bibles, in the Hebrew Old Testament they are one—Ezra–Nehemiah. The style suggests they were written by one author, and they tell a single story of return and rebuilding after exile, with Ezra as an important figure throughout.

Ezra–Nehemiah (as we will call it) tells the story of three waves of exiled Jews returning to the Promised Land, the construction of a second temple to replace the first, and the building of walls around Jerusalem for protection. Jason S. DeRouchie and Daryl Aaron note, "The events recorded in this book span almost a century, running from around 538 B.C. when Cyrus decreed that the Jewish exiles could return to the Promised Land, through the return under Ezra just after Esther (458 B.C.), and into the governorship of Nehemiah, which began in 444 B.C."[1] But the message of this book is also like my east coast vacation: Although there were many real blessings and displays of YHWH's faithfulness, there was also a nagging sense of disappointment that there had to be something more.

A GLORIOUS PROCLAMATION BY A LESS-THAN-GLORIOUS KING

Ezra–Nehemiah begins with a glorious proclamation by King Cyrus of Persia at a time when his kingdom was the new superpower of the ancient world. Cyrus was in the first year of his reign, and his approach was quite different from the Babylonians he had defeated. Instead of employing force and power to beat his subjects into submission, he used *kindness* to *win* their allegiance. YHWH had promised through the prophet Jeremiah that after seventy years, the exiled Jews would be able to return and rebuild (see Jer 29:10). The glorious proclamation at the beginning of Ezra–Nehemiah, then, is a display of YHWH's faithfulness to keep his promises:

> In the first year of Cyrus king of Persia, that the word of the LORD by the mouth of Jeremiah might be fulfilled, the LORD stirred up the spirit of Cyrus king of Persia, so that he made a proclamation throughout all his kingdom and also put it in writing:
>
> "Thus says Cyrus king of Persia: The LORD, the God of heaven, has given me all the kingdoms of the earth, and he has charged me to build him a house at Jerusalem, which is in Judah. Whoever is among you of all his people, may his God be with him, and let him go up to Jerusalem, which is in Judah, and rebuild the house of the LORD, the God

[1]Jason S. DeRouchie and Daryl Aaron, "Ezra–Nehemiah," in *What the Old Testament Authors Really Cared About: A Survey of Jesus' Bible*, ed. Jason S. DeRouchie (Kregel Academic, 2013), 428.

> of Israel—he is the God who is in Jerusalem. And let each survivor, in whatever place he sojourns, be assisted by the men of his place with silver and gold, with goods and with beasts, besides freewill offerings for the house of God that is in Jerusalem." (Ezra 1:1-4)

What a miracle.

At first glance, Cyrus sounds like a convert to YHWH. His spirit was stirred up by YHWH, which led him to make this proclamation (Ezra 1:1). He also gave YHWH credit for his possession of all the kingdoms of the earth (Ezra 1:2). He was even sensitive to prompting by this same God to build him a house in Jerusalem (Ezra 1:2). In response, Cyrus then commissioned the exiled Jews to return to their land and rebuild their temple. We can imagine the surprise and joy of the Jewish people when the newest—and much bigger—world superpower gave them back their very valuable articles for temple worship, proclaiming that they could return to their land, rebuild their temple, and worship their God again.

This positive reading of Cyrus seems to be strengthened by the prophet Isaiah, who reports the words of YHWH, "who says of Cyrus, 'He is my shepherd, and he shall fulfill all my purpose'; saying of Jerusalem, 'She shall be built,' and of the temple, 'Your foundation shall be laid'" (Is 44:28). This prophecy refers to the Persian king Cyrus as *YHWH's shepherd who fulfills YHWH's purpose* of rebuilding Jerusalem and its temple. No wonder the same prophet later calls Cyrus YHWH's *anointed one*—his messiah (see Is 45:1).

But who was this man, and what moved him to issue such a proclamation? Karen Jobes helps with the historical context:

> Cyrus II (the Great) . . . conquered the Babylonian empire without a battle when his army entered Babylon by wading up the Euphrates river and through the canals of the city on the night of October 12, 539 B.C. . . . Cyrus was welcomed as a liberator by the inhabitants of Babylon, and the vast lands previously ruled by the Babylonian kings,

> including Jerusalem and Judah, became part of the expanding Persian empire.[2]

No wonder he was called Cyrus the Great.

What about Cyrus's religious allegiances? As we look more closely at the Bible's portrait of Cyrus, it is clear that he was a foreign king used by YHWH to accomplish his purposes. However, Isaiah's description of Cyrus adds that YHWH accomplished these things through the Persian king *even though Cyrus did not know YHWH* (Is 45:4).[3] This is also confirmed subtly in Ezra 1:3, where Cyrus refers to YHWH as "the God who is in Jerusalem." As Robert Alter puts it, "Here Cyrus sounds more like a polytheist, assuming there are different local gods."[4] YHWH could use an evil king with his less-than-wholesome motives to accomplish his purposes. In fact, he had just accomplished his purposes of bringing curses on his covenant-breaking people through the leadership of the evil Babylonian king Nebuchadnezzar, whom YHWH even called *his servant* (see Jer 25:9; 27:6; 43:10). Although Nebuchadnezzar was a wicked king, he did whatever YHWH's plan had predestined to take place (see Herod and Pontius Pilate in Acts 4:28).

This more negative understanding of Cyrus is confirmed by ancient historical records, which present him as a master at military victory as well as one who organized and won over those under his rule. Archaeologists have discovered a clay cylinder written in an ancient script that documents the annals of Cyrus's rule.[5] Cyrus's policies as described in this ancient artifact record his dealings with the many nations he conquered: "According to it, he released many people

---

[2]Karen H. Jobes, *Esther*, New International Version Application Commentary (Zondervan Academic, 1999), 23.

[3]I was first alerted to this by Bruce K. Waltke and Charles Yu, *An Old Testament Theology: An Exegetical, Canonical, and Thematic Approach* (Zondervan, 2007), 796.

[4]Robert Alter, *The Hebrew Bible: A Translation with Commentary* (Norton, 2019), 3:807.

[5]This fascinating artifact is currently housed in the British Museum. The script is called cuneiform.

groups held captive by the Babylonian kings, and he organized and financed their return to their homelands. . . . In addition to the temple at Jerusalem, Cyrus restored and repaired pagan temples in Uruk, Ur, and Babylon."[6]

This means that Cyrus's decree in Ezra 1:1-4 was not unique. He did the same thing with the other nations in his vast kingdom. But the exact quotation of this Cyrus cylinder is even more revealing: "By [Marduk's] exalted [word], . . . I returned the (images of) the gods to the sacred centers [on the other side of] the Tigris whose sanctuaries had been abandoned for a long time, and I let them dwell in eternal abodes. I gathered all their inhabitants and returned (to them) their dwellings."[7] According to this historical artifact, what Cyrus attributed to the (so-called) god Marduk, the Bible attributes to YHWH, the God of heaven (see Ezra 1:2; 2 Chron 36:23).[8]

As we consider the data, it becomes clear that it was a *political strategy* for Cyrus to allow various people groups—the Jews included—to return to their homelands and worship their own gods. By sending them to their original homes, Cyrus strengthened his authority in the farthest parts of his empire, and he also established the loyalty of his subjects. Even though the various exiled people groups (including the Jews) could return to their homelands, they were still subjects of Persia. Far from being a convert to YHWH, Cyrus was a pagan political strategist. In fact, as Andrew Hill notes, "He sought to placate the gods of these people groups by encouraging the traditional worship of local deities."[9]

In light of these insights, how are we to interpret the Bible's teaching about Cyrus? Through the lens of the sovereignty of God. Ezra puts

---

[6]See Jobes, *Esther*, 24-25.

[7]As cited in DeRouchie and Aaron, "Ezra–Nehemiah," 432, citing a translation from William W. Hallo, ed., *The Context of Scripture* (Brill, 1997–2002), 315.28-36; cf. James B. Pritchard, ed., *Ancient Near Eastern Texts Relating to the Old Testament*, 3rd ed. (Princeton University Press, 1969), 316.

[8]See DeRouchie and Aaron, "Ezra–Nehemiah," 432.

[9]Andrew E. Hill, *1 & 2 Chronicles*, New International Version Application Commentary (Zondervan, 2003), 652.

it like this: "Our God has not forsaken us in our slavery, but has extended to us his steadfast love before the kings of Persia, to grant us some reviving to set up the house of our God, to repair its ruins, and to give us protection in Judea and Jerusalem" (Ezra 9:9). By saying this, Ezra was not burying his head in the sand, nor was he revising history to suit his purposes. As another author phrases it, "We see in Scripture time and time again how God works through anyone he pleases."[10] Although Cyrus was an opportunistic, kingdom-expanding, political strategist, the Bible teaches that he was a puppet in the hand of the God of heaven—the very one who made and rules the world.

A GLORIOUS SECOND REDEMPTION

On a macro level, Ezra–Nehemiah tells the glorious story of three waves of return from exile—what the Bible also presents as a new (or second) exodus.[11] These three waves of return occurred over a nearly one-hundred-year period—from the first in 538 BC to the third in 444 BC. Over these years, four Persian kings reigned: Cyrus, Darius, Ahasuerus, and Artaxerxes (see Ezra 4:5-7). As Waltke summarizes, "Each return culminates in a different project of reconstruction: building of the temple (Ezra 1–6), basing the community on the Mosaic law (Ezra 7–10), and building the walls of Jerusalem (Neh. 1:1–7:3)."[12] And Ezra–Nehemiah makes clear that all of the blessings it records were from the gracious hand of God.

Ezra 1–6 tells the story of the first return, in 538 BC, led by the governors Sheshbazzar and his nephew Zerubbabel along with Jeshua the priest. These men are sent back to their homeland with finances from the Persian king and with the sacred vessels for temple worship

[10]Peter E. Enns, *Exodus*, New International Version Application Commentary (Zondervan Academic, 2000), 75.

[11]Many details for this section were gleaned from the summary chart in DeRouchie and Aaron, "Ezra–Nehemiah," 431.

[12]Waltke and Yu, *Old Testament Theology*, 775.

that King Nebuchadnezzar of Babylon took when he defeated Jerusalem. This was a very dangerous journey with 5,400 gold and silver objects that needed to return to Jerusalem for worship in the second temple (Ezra 1:11). Although up to one hundred thousand Jews had been taken into exile, we learn from the detailed records in this book that 49,697 people (including servants) returned to Jerusalem along with these leaders (see Ezra 2:64-65).[13] During this time, temple rebuilding began, sacrifices were offered again, and the Feast of Booths was celebrated (see Lev 23:43).[14] Matthew Levering helps us to understand, "Because it truly is a new exodus . . . their first celebration in the land is the feast of booths."[15]

Next, Ezra 8–10 tells the story of a second return under Ezra, whom we learn is "a scribe skilled in the Law of Moses that the LORD, the God of Israel, had given" (Ezra 7:6). But he is also called "Ezra the priest, the scribe, a man learned in matters of the commandments of the LORD and his statutes for Israel" (Ezra 7:11). This means that he was both a priest (who mediated between YHWH and his people) and a scribe (a biblical scholar). We also learn that Ezra was a descendant of Aaron, the first high priest (Ezra 7:1-5). As Waltke says, "As a descendant of Aaron, Ezra is genealogically qualified for the task of reconstructing the community on the basis of Mosaic law. Unquestionably the restored Israel is a continuation of the old."[16]

This second wave of return took place eighty years after the first, in 458 BC. As with the first return, any Jew could return to Jerusalem. The detailed records in this book reveal that 1,754 people returned with Ezra, including men, Levites, and helpers (see Ezra 8:1-20). This time was marked by temple worship, along with repairs and

---

[13]See Waltke and Yu, *Old Testament Theology*, 772.

[14]As a descendant of David, Zerubabbel was authorized to rebuild the temple (see 2 Sam 7). Thanks to Jonny Atkinson for pointing me to this link (personal correspondence).

[15]Matthew Levering, *Ezra & Nehemiah*, Brazos Theological Commentary on the Bible (Brazos, 2023), 52.

[16]Waltke and Yu, *Old Testament Theology*, 782.

restorations that were partly financed by Persia, as before. Even though there was still no king on David's throne—the king of Persia still ruled God's people—they were allowed to install civil magistrates at this time (see Ezra 7:6-26).

In Nehemiah 1:1–7:3, a third return (with an unknown number of people) occurs in 444 BC, under the leadership of Nehemiah, who was cupbearer to the king of Persia. Far from being a menial role, Waltke explains, "The royal cupbearer tastes the king's wine (to prevent poisoning), guards the royal chambers, and comforts the king. As such he becomes the most trusted official and enjoys influence with his master."[17] This trust goes a long way as Nehemiah is allowed to rebuild the Jerusalem city walls and gates with partial financing from the Persians yet again. These are rebuilt in only fifty-two days, even in the face of enemy opposition (see Neh 6:15).

Finally, Nehemiah 7:4–13:31 shares a theme with Ezra 9–10: "renewal and reformations of the restored congregation."[18] At this time Ezra the scribe/priest reads from the Book of the Law (i.e., God's Word). As a result, the community rejoices, the Feast of Booths is celebrated, the community confesses their sins, the covenant is renewed, the wall is dedicated, and other reforms take place.

These events were nothing short of spectacular. During a period of roughly one hundred years, the city of Jerusalem was restored, worship was reinstituted at a second temple, Old Testament feasts were celebrated again, and the city was protected with proper walls. God's people also renewed the covenant and recommitted themselves to his Word. They repented of their sins in very practical ways, and they showed absolute commitment to their God. Over this period, at least 51,451 Jewish people returned to Jerusalem and its surrounding region, not including the unknown number who returned in the third wave. These events were clear displays of YHWH's faithfulness, but

---

[17]Waltke and Yu, *Old Testament Theology*, 786.

[18]Waltke and Yu, *Old Testament Theology*, 775.

they also left God's people yearning for something more. They had fallen short of the ultimate redemption that had been promised by the Old Testament prophets.

GLORIOUS BUT NOT ULTIMATE

So far we have noticed that the blessings experienced in Ezra–Nehemiah were according to God's promises to bring restoration for covenant repentance (see Deut 30:1-10). We would think that, when the altar was rebuilt and the foundation of the temple was laid (Ezra 3), the entire community would rejoice. But while the returnees had hoped that this would usher in the full restoration, Ezra 3 signals that it was only a first step. Although the Jews in Ezra 3 are already experiencing massive blessings from YHWH, they are not yet experiencing the fullness.

The first hint at this comes in the celebration at the laying of the temple's foundation. This scene reports shouts of joy:

> And when the builders laid the foundation of the temple of the LORD, the priests in their vestments came forward with trumpets, and the Levites, the sons of Asaph, with cymbals, to praise the LORD, according to the directions of David king of Israel. And they sang responsively, praising and giving thanks to the LORD,
>
> "For he is good,
> for his steadfast love endures forever toward Israel."
>
> And all the people shouted with a great shout when they praised the LORD, because the foundation of the house of the LORD was laid. (Ezra 3:10-11)

However, joy is not the only loud sound on this occasion: "But many of the priests and Levites and heads of fathers' houses, old men who had seen the first house, wept with a loud voice when they saw the foundation of this house being laid" (Ezra 3:12). In fact, shouts of joy and sorrow are happening at the same time, "so that the people could not distinguish the sound of the joyful shout from the sound of the people's weeping, for the people shouted with a great shout, and the sound was heard far away" (Ezra 3:13).

What was going on here? The younger generation overflowed with joy to YHWH, singing the same refrain that was sung when the ark was brought into the first temple: "For he is good, for his steadfast love endures forever toward Israel" (Ezra 3:11; cf. Ps 106:1; 107:1; 118:1, 29; 136:1; see 2 Chron 5:13). But at the same time, the older men wept as they sang something more like Bono's haunting refrain that he still hasn't found what he's looking for. This was not because the older men were hard to please. The book of Ezra tells us that *they had seen the first temple*—the one that had been destroyed by the Babylonians—and this second temple was a disappointment.

While the prophets had been prophesying that the new, restored temple would be *bigger and more glorious* than the first (see especially Ezek 40–48), this temple was smaller and less glorious. Waltke adds that the offerings of the returnees paled in comparison to Solomon's offerings at the dedication of the first temple.[19] Derek Kidner adds further, "This time there is no ark, no visible glory, indeed no Temple: only some beginnings, and small beginnings at that."[20]

In fact, the most common designation for the land of Israel in Ezra–Nehemiah is "the province beyond the river" (see Ezra 4:10-11, 16-17, 20; 5:3, 6; 6:6, 13; 7:21, 25; 8:36; Neh 2:7, 9; 3:7). Although it may be easy for our eyes to skim over this designation, it would have sent chills down the spines of the first readers of Ezra–Nehemiah. Why? Because it would have been a reminder that there was no *land* of Israel at all: They may have returned to their *geographical* homeland, but it was now a province in the vast kingdom of Persia.[21] Far from being its own country with a descendant of David reigning on the throne,

[19]See Waltke and Yu, *Old Testament Theology*, 780.

[20]Derek Kidner, *Ezra and Nehemiah*, Tyndale Old Testament Commentary (InterVarsity Press, 2009), 53.

[21]This is reinforced in Esther 1:1, which speaks of the Persian Empire as consisting of 127 provinces.

Judah had become the Persian province of Yehud, ruled by a Persian king who had set up his own governors.

The older men were weeping because this temple did "not yet" represent the full fulfillment of YHWH's promises to his people through the prophets. The blessings in Ezra–Nehemiah were real and good and from the hand of YHWH, but there was still more to come. As House puts it,

> The people have made a start, yet the whole of Jerusalem is not holy to the Lord (Zech 14:20), the Davidic ruler is not in place (Jer 33:14-18), the people's hearts are not wholly changed (Ezek 36:26-27), and evildoers are not yet eradicated (Dan 9:24-27). Short-term promises are being kept now, but long-term, permanent solutions to Israel's problems await completion. The canon indicates that more will be done by the God who governs human events.[22]

Ezra–Nehemiah tells the story of a second redemption that is only partly accomplished. The fullness is yet to come.

RESPONDING TO YHWH'S WORD

Although Ezra–Nehemiah leaves the reader yearning for something more, this book also represents a glorious beginning. Not only does this book record three waves of return, but it also revels in the people's radical recommitment to God's Word. For example, Ezra is described as a scribe/priest who "had set his heart to study the Law of the Lord, and to do it and to teach his statutes and rules in Israel" (Ezra 7:10). This devotion plays out in a few key scenes.

In Ezra 9, we encounter a model prayer of community repentance, resulting in concrete displays of radical commitment to YHWH.[23] The story of the community's drastic measures related to this commitment is told in the next chapter.

---

[22]Paul R. House, *Old Testament Theology* (InterVarsity Press, 1998), 519. For similar sentiments, see James M. Hamilton Jr., *God's Glory in Salvation Through Judgment: A Biblical Theology* (Crossway, 2010), 323.

[23]Neh 9 also records a model prayer of repentance.

When most readers encounter Ezra 10, they are bewildered. How could a mass divorce be anything but tragic? At the beginning of Ezra 9, some officials report to him:

> The people of Israel and the priests and the Levites have not separated themselves from the peoples of the lands with their abominations, from the Canaanites, the Hittites, the Perizzites, the Jebusites, the Ammonites, the Moabites, the Egyptians, and the Amorites. For they have taken some of their daughters to be wives for themselves and for their sons, so that the holy race has mixed itself with the peoples of the lands. And in this faithlessness the hand of the officials and chief men has been foremost. (Ezra 9:1-2)

Ezra responds by tearing his clothes, pulling out his hair, and sitting appalled until the evening sacrifice, when he falls on his knees, spreads out his hands to YHWH his God, and leads a long prayer of public confession (Ezra 9:3-15). In response, the community as a whole weeps bitterly, because they "married foreign women from the peoples of the land" (Ezra 10:2). Since this is a great sin that cannot be undone overnight (see Ezra 10:13), the people begin the long and messy process of divorcing their foreign wives.

How should we understand this disturbing scene?[24] First, remember that according to the Bible, divorce is always tragic, even when permissible, because one spouse has broken the marriage covenant (see, e.g., Mt 19:9; 1 Cor 7:15). In marriage, God takes two people and creates one out of them; even in instances of the most horrible abuse or the most heinous adultery, divorce always hurts, because it tears apart a couple that God joined together (see Mt 19:6).[25] Ezra 10 is not

---

[24]I am thankful to Tricia Versteeg for her helpful feedback on these sensitive paragraphs about divorce in Ezra 10.

[25]Since every person's situation is unique, care should be taken to discern every individual case of potential divorce with local church elders and other wise counselors. For example, this is emphatically not to say that someone should stay in a situation where their life or the lives of their children are in danger because divorce hurts; sometimes the pain of staying would far outweigh the pain of divorce and may even endanger others.

making light of divorce. In fact, it presents the sin of God's people as so great that it requires this mass tragedy as part of its repentance.

Second, Ezra 10 does not condone ethnic elitism. The Bible is filled with examples of non-Jews marrying Jews. In fact, "the high priest was the only Israelite not allowed to marry a foreigner (Lev. 21:14), in contrast to other priests and cultic officials (21:7)."[26] And as we saw in chapter six, in Matthew 1:1-17 the New Testament *celebrates* four non-Jewish women in *Jesus'* lineage: Tamar the Canaanite, Rahab (the prostitute from Jericho), Ruth the Moabite, and Bathsheba (who had been the wife of Uriah the Hittite). Each of these women is a reminder that God's people extended far beyond ethnic Israel and that the gospel of Jesus Christ must be preached to all nations, to the end of the earth (see Mt 28:18-20; Acts 1:8). In fact, in Ezra 6:21, we are told that the Passover meal "was eaten by the people of Israel who had returned from exile, and also by every one who had joined them and separated himself from the uncleanness of the peoples of the land to worship the LORD, the God of Israel" (Ezra 6:21). And then in Nehemiah 10:28, the community pledge to follow the Torah of Moses is made by the same two groups: Jews and non-Jews who had committed themselves to YHWH.[27] Therefore, foreignness is not the problem in Ezra 10.

So what is the issue? Köstenberger and Goswell point out that the concern of Ezra 9–10 is "foreign wives who retain their foreign ways (Neh. 13:23-24)."[28] Over and over again in the Old Testament, when a leader in Israel marries a foreigner, the gods of that foreigner corrupt the leader and the nation (see Solomon). For this reason, Gary Schnittjer and Matthew Harmon write, "Isaiah, Ezekiel, and Ezra–Nehemiah each

---

[26]Andreas J. Köstenberger and Gregory Goswell, *Biblical Theology: A Canonical, Thematic, and Ethical Approach* (Crossway, 2023), 328.

[27]I first made the link between these references and Ezra 10 in reading Köstenberger and Goswell, *Biblical Theology*, 339; and Gary Edward Schnittjer and Matthew S. Harmon, *How to Study the Bible's Use of the Bible: Seven Hermeneutical Choices for the Old and New Testaments* (Zondervan Academic, 2024), 3-4.

[28]Köstenberger and Goswell, *Biblical Theology*, 328.

promote two kinds of others—excluded others and included others—in continuity with the same twofold teaching in Torah."[29] Throughout the Old Testament, excluded others threaten the purity of God's people, while included others turn from their sinful ways and wholly commit themselves to YHWH. As Waltke puts it, the marriages in Ezra 10 threaten to steal Israel's heart away from loyalty to YHWH.[30] The ultimate goal of Ezra 10 is a fledgling but pure community that is wholly devoted to YHWH.

Finally, this is a time-specific occurrence. Köstenberger and Goswell explain:

> The perceived moral problem may be eased in part by consideration of the extenuating circumstances of the times: the religious vulnerability of the people of God, without clear territorial integrity as part of the Persian empire, made such rigor necessary if Israelite identity was to survive at all. The argument is, then, that the drastic measures taken are to be seen as a response to contemporary issues.[31]

Therefore, Ezra 9–10 is not normative. In fact, the New Testament teaches that when a Christian is married to a nonbeliever, they should remain married and seek to win that spouse to Christ (see, e.g., 1 Cor 7:12-16; 1 Pet 3:1-7). The point for our purposes is that the community was willing to take a radical step of repentance, despite how painful it must have been.

Before we close our chapter by looking forward to Christ, let's remind ourselves of two key truths about Ezra–Nehemiah: (1) This book marks a glorious *beginning*, as it displays the faithfulness of YHWH to *begin* the process of restoration; and (2) this book also falls short of the ultimate goal. Put differently, seeds of the great second

---

[29]Schnittjer and Harmon, *How to Study the Bible's Use of the Bible*, 3. In n7 on the same page, they list the following references: excluded others (Ex 12:45; Deut 23:3-6; Is 52:1; Ezek 44:9; Ezra 4:1, 4; Neh 10:30); included others (Ex 12:48-49; Deut 23:7-8; Isa 56:3-7; Ezek 14:7; 47:22-23; Ezra 6:21; Neh 10:28).

[30]See Waltke and Yu, *Old Testament Theology*, 785.

[31]Köstenberger and Goswell, *Biblical Theology*, 327.

redemption are planted, and they even germinate, but the fullness of this great restoration is still far in the future. As James M. Hamilton Jr. says, "The people returned to the land but not to Eden. They are 'already' back in the land, but they have 'not yet' seen the desert bloom, Jerusalem exalted over every other mountain, and the nations streaming to Zion."[32] For this reason, the Old Testament doesn't conclude with Ezra–Nehemiah but with Chronicles, a book that looks forward with eager anticipation to the ultimate redemption that will be fully accomplished by Jesus Christ. We'll unpack this idea more fully in chapter nine.

LOOKING FORWARD TO CHRIST: "YOU HAVE HEARD IT SAID . . . BUT I SAY TO YOU"

As we conclude by looking forward to Christ, let's turn back to an amazing scene from Nehemiah 8. In this chapter, all the people gather and call on Ezra the scribe-priest to bring "the Book of the Law of Moses that the Lord had commanded Israel" (Neh 8:1). Ezra reads from God's word from early morning until midday—about six hours. Far from complaining about a long-winded preacher, "the ears of all the people were attentive to the Book of the Law" (Neh 8:3). They are *hungry* to hear God's word and to do it. As Ezra opens the word of God, the people *stand* (for six hours!) and then bless YHWH. The people answer, "Amen, Amen," and lift their hands and bow their heads to worship YHWH with their faces to the ground (Neh 8:6). Other readers help Ezra during this six-hour event while the people remain in their places (Neh 8:7). Then "they read from the book, from the Law of God, clearly, and they gave the sense, so that the people understood the reading" (Neh 8:8). Although the meaning "giving the sense" is debated, I favor the idea of "explaining" the Word of God, much like today's preachers do in their Sunday sermons.[33] In this

---

[32]Hamilton, *God's Glory in Salvation Through Judgment*, 323.

[33]For an extended discussion of translation possibilities, with the same conclusion I have drawn, see W. Hall Harris, ed., *The NET Bible Notes* (Biblical Studies Press, 2005), Nehemiah 8:8, n10.

six-hour scene, a spiritually hungry community is being shaped by the Old Testament Scriptures through the ministry of faithful teachers of God's Word. Most importantly, the people understand what they are hearing (Neh 8:12).

As we come to the New Testament, we discover that Jesus also taught large crowds, but he was greater than Ezra the scribe or any of his associates. He was even greater than Moses, from whose books Ezra taught. Moses wrote God's Word as the greatest Old Testament prophet (Deut 34:10-12), and centuries later Ezra and his associates read and taught from those same books. In the New Testament we encounter Jesus as a better preacher than Ezra and a better lawgiver than Moses.

By Matthew 5, Jesus has been baptized, filled with the Holy Spirit, and identified as the beloved Son of God (Mt 3:16-17). He has also proven himself faithful in his wilderness temptations, where he used the word of God to combat the devil's schemes (Mt 4:1-11). He has begun his public ministry, called his first disciples, and ministered to great crowds. When he sees the crowds, Jesus goes up on the mountain (Mt 5:1). He sits down, and his disciples come to him. And then he teaches with authority. While Moses reported God's words and while Ezra read them and gave their sense, Jesus reveals the depth of their application to Christians, who are filled with the Holy Spirit. The previous covenant was given through Moses and was returned to through covenant repentance under the ministries of scribe-priests such as Ezra, but it didn't ultimately and enduringly penetrate the hard hearts of the community. However, the Old Testament prophets promised that the new covenant would be marked by a people whose hearts of stone would be replaced with hearts of flesh (Ezek 36:26), who would have YHWH's instruction written on their hearts (Jer 31:31-34), and who would all be filled with YHWH's Spirit (Joel 2:28-32). So, as Jesus ushers in this new covenant era, he also intensifies the covenant's demands. Unlike under the old covenant, new covenant believers in Jesus will have the power to change from the inside out.

One example of such powerful living is found in Matthew 5:21-48. In this portion of his great sermon, Jesus touches on lust, divorce, oaths, retaliation, and how to respond to one's enemies. Each time, he begins with "You have heard that it was said" and continues with "but I say to you." In each case, Jesus teaches that true conformity to God's perfect standards must come from the heart. In these statements, Jesus accomplishes two things: He corrects inaccurate interpretations of the Old Testament by the Jewish teachers of his day, and he shows his followers how to interpret the Old Testament now that he is fulfilling it (see Mt 5:17). D. A. Carson explains:

> The contrast between what the people had heard and what Jesus taught is not based on distinctions like casuistry versus love, outer legalism versus inner commitment, or even false interpretation versus true interpretation, though all of them impinge collaterally on the text. Rather, in every case Jesus contrasts the people's misunderstanding of the law with the true direction in which the law points, according to his own authority as the law's "fulfiller" (in the sense established in v. 17).[34]

For example, it is not enough to simply keep from committing adultery, because Jesus teaches that "everyone who looks at a woman with lustful intent has already committed adultery with her in his heart" (Mt 5:28). He then goes on to teach about taking radical measures to kill sin in our heart. No wonder the crowds are amazed at his authority (see Mt 7:28-29).[35]

The lesson we can draw from this is wonderful: God's Word is precious, and there was a very real sense that Ezra's six-hour sermon was a wonderful blessing (Neh 8). But how much more is the teaching of Jesus an even greater blessing, for new covenant Christians hear his teaching with soft hearts, ready to be shaped by what he says. I praise

---

[34]D. A. Carson, "Matthew," in *Matthew, Mark, Luke*, ed. Tremper Longman III and David E. Garland, The Expositor's Bible Commentary 9 (Zondervan Academic, 1984), 148.

[35]I was first alerted to this link by Carson, "Matthew," 148.

God that since Jesus fulfilled the Old Testament, we are given new hearts and new power to change from the inside out.

DISCUSSION QUESTIONS

1. What does the Bible say about Cyrus's motives for allowing the Jews to return to their land and to build their temple? How is this portrait confirmed by archaeological evidence?
2. What are some other biblical examples of God using a wicked human ruler to accomplish his purposes?
3. How does Deuteronomy 30:1-10 help us understand Ezra–Nehemiah?
4. What are some of the key, glorious blessings that God's people experienced in Ezra–Nehemiah?
5. What are some specific ways that the blessings in Ezra–Nehemiah fell short of the past glory experienced by God's people as well as the greater glory promised by the Old Testament prophets?
6. What are some key responses of community repentance recorded in Ezra–Nehemiah? Should Christians today follow all these practices?
7. How is Jesus a better, more powerful preacher than Ezra the scribe-priest?

HOPE

THE ULTIMATE REDEMPTION FULLY ACCOMPLISHED

We have finally arrived at the hope-filled conclusion of the Old Testament story. As we saw in the present book's introduction, if we are going to get the most out of Chronicles, we need to follow Jesus' lead. This means that we should read the Old Testament in its earliest attested Hebrew order, with Genesis first and Chronicles last. As we do this, the message of Chronicles will pop off the page and into our hearts.

When we encounter Chronicles as the climax of the Old Testament story, we discover a hope-filled book that sums up the history from Adam to the return from exile and looks forward with anticipation to a bigger and better restoration to come. The author begins with Adam (1 Chron 1:1) and concludes with King Cyrus's decree that the exiled Jews can return to their homeland to rebuild their temple (2 Chron 36:23). For these reasons, Jerome's fourth- or fifth-century AD description of this book has appropriately stuck: "a chronicle of the whole divine history."[1]

Todd Bolen digs a bit more into the big-picture story of Chronicles:

> The first nine chapters provide the genealogies. The next twenty-nine chapters describe the seventy-three years when David and Solomon

[1]Andrew E. Hill and John H. Walton, *A Survey of the Old Testament*, 4th ed. (Zondervan Academic, 2023), 215.

> ruled from Jerusalem during the united monarchy. The last twenty-seven chapters survey all 345 years of the kingdom of Judah. Of the reigns of David and Solomon, eighteen chapters focus on the temple planning and construction. Of the kings that followed, the Chronicler regarded their treatment of the temple as a "weathervane" of their relationship to Yahweh.[2]

In this chapter we will walk through the hope-filled message of Chronicles in four points: genealogy, David, temple, and hope. Then we'll conclude as we have done in each of this book's chapters: by looking forward from Chronicles to Christ.

GENEALOGY (1 CHRON 1–9)

If you wanted to write a *New York Times* bestselling book, how would you begin your story?[3] I suspect that none of us would even think of beginning with a genealogy and that no publisher today would even entertain such a book proposal. But things were different in Old Testament Israel: For this particular group of readers, a nine-chapter genealogy was the perfect way to draw them into the story.

The genealogy begins with the first man, Adam, from the story of creation in Genesis 1–2. In a very real sense, Chronicles is a summary of the Old Testament story, beginning at the very beginning.

This genealogy is not generic: It shows that "the Lord is the God who has chosen Israel from the very creation of the human race (1 Chron 1:1–9:34)."[4] House adds,

> The Chronicler utilizes the genealogical material from Genesis in 1:1–2:2. Elements of Genesis 5:1-32, 10:1-32, 11:10-26, 25:12-18, 35:23-26 and 36:1-43 appear. . . . [This] shows that the Chronicler considers the lives of Abraham, Isaac and Jacob the capstone of early human history. All

[2]Todd Bolen, "1–2 Chronicles," in *What the Old Testament Authors Really Cared About: A Survey of Jesus' Bible*, ed. Jason S. DeRouchie (Kregel Academic, 2013), 448.
[3]I first heard this illustration from Keith Bodner.
[4]Paul R. House, *Old Testament Theology* (InterVarsity Press, 1998), 524.

> that precedes their times is a prelude to the important work God does in and through their lives.[5]

According to Chronicles, Israel's story is the most important aspect of world history. In fact, Israelite tribes outside the Southern Kingdom of Judah are included in this number. For example, 1 Chronicles 9:3 reveals, "And some of the people of Judah, Benjamin, Ephraim, and Manasseh lived in Jerusalem." While it may be easy for our eyes to skim over these details, the first readers of Chronicles would have been stunned. Recall that after the death of Solomon, the kingdom was split in two, with the Southern Kingdom of Judah and the Northern Kingdom of Israel. But the tribes listed in 1 Chronicles 9:3 indicate that the author of Chronicles thought of Israel as one united people.[6]

The apex of this nine-chapter genealogy also adds to its story. While the genealogies in Genesis have Abraham as their climax, the genealogy in Chronicles focuses on someone else. Bolen explains: "From the start, the Chronicler focused on David, as he traced the genealogy from Adam to Abraham and from Abraham to the twelve tribes (ch. 1). The first tribal genealogy he gave was not that of the oldest, Reuben, or even of Joseph, who had the rights of the firstborn, but of Judah, from whom the royal redeemer was to rise (2:1–5:2; cf. Gen. 49:10)."[7]

Why is this? Since David was the promised king whose dynasty would lead God's people to the Messiah, his lineage was vital. So the author of Chronicles focuses on that lineage "to assure the exiles that the House of David lives."[8] Since David's dynasty was very much alive, so were the hopes of its first readers, the Jews who had returned from exile.

---

[5]House, *Old Testament Theology*, 525.

[6]See Andreas J. Köstenberger and Gregory Goswell, *Biblical Theology: A Canonical, Thematic, and Ethical Approach* (Crossway, 2023), 329; Bruce K. Waltke and Charles Yu, *An Old Testament Theology: An Exegetical, Canonical, and Thematic Approach* (Zondervan, 2007), 756.

[7]Bolen, "1–2 Chronicles," 444.

[8]Waltke and Yu, *Old Testament Theology*, 759.

Finally, the nine-chapter genealogy in Chronicles was very personal for the first readers of this book because it led to *them*. Since the book's first readers were part of this grand lineage, God's promises of restoration for covenant repentance applied to *them* (see Deut 30:1-10). As they experienced the first fruits of that promised restoration, this genealogy assured them that they could place all their hope in the rock-solid promises of full and ultimate restoration because these promises were written for *them*.

Although we as readers today may not be gripped by a nine-chapter genealogy, we can start to see just how practical it really was if we slip into the sandals of this book's first readers. This genealogy points to hope for the world through the restoration of God's people and the reemergence of a king on David's throne.

DAVID (1 CHRON 9:35–29:30)

Since David is the focal point of the first nine chapters of Chronicles, we should not be surprised that he is also the focus of the nineteen chapters that come next: After the author traced David's lineage, he tells David's story. In fact, this section of Chronicles *begins* with the death of Saul. We learn not only *that* King Saul died but also *why* he died: "for his breach of faith" (1 Chron 10:13). Since Israel's first king was not YHWH's chosen covenant partner, David will be the focus of Chronicles. This shows that though Chronicles was written for Jewish readers who already knew the story of Samuel–Kings, they needed a special message *for them* in their situation of embarking on a return from exile. As Dempster puts it,

> Just as in Genesis the goal of history could be clarified by studying the genealogies (history starts with the arrival of Abraham), so too all the genealogies in Chronicles end when David arrives on the historical scene. The capture of Jerusalem and David's reign are the focus of the next nineteen chapters. Again, it is as if all history has been waiting, not in this case, for Abraham, but for David from the tribe of Judah.

> Or, in the words of Brueggemann . . . , all history is regarded as a footnote to David.[9]

The story of David is told with two emphases, and neither of these are the focus in Samuel–Kings. First, Chronicles provides many extra details about David's role in temple worship. Although the construction of the temple was reserved for Solomon, Paul House adds,

> Not only does David collect the materials for the temple (22:2-19; 29:1-9), but he also sets the duties of the Levites (23:1-32), the priests (24:1-31), the musicians (25:1-31) and the gatekeepers (26:1-19). In every possible way, David undergirds the work of worship, thereby proving himself the sort of ideal king described in Moses' initial standards for kings (Deut 17:14-20).[10]

In light of this, Bolen is correct that "this book is really about these two houses—how God raised up the Davidic *dynasty* as a beacon of hope and how David's royal house constructed and maintained Yahweh's *temple*."[11]

The other difference is what Chronicles does not focus on: many of David's sins. The David of Chronicles is far from perfect—for example, he is incited by Satan to take a census that results in the discipline of YHWH on the community (1 Chron 21:1). But his grave sins against Bathsheba and Uriah are not even reported. Was the author whitewashing the story of David? Bolen explains: "The writer is almost silent regarding the king's faults, choosing instead to focus on God's promises to David and the king's faithful obedience. Because David's sins with Bathsheba and Uriah do not contribute to these emphases, the Chronicler did not repeat the sad stories of 2 Samuel."[12] Far from whitewashing David's life story, the author of Chronicles emphasizes

---

[9]Stephen G. Dempster, *Dominion and Dynasty*, New Studies in Biblical Theology 18 (InterVarsity Press, 2004), 226. See also Dempster, *The Return of the Kingdom: A Biblical Theology of God's Reign* (IVP Academic, 2024), 150.

[10]House, *Old Testament Theology*, 528.

[11]Bolen, "1–2 Chronicles," 444, emphasis original.

[12]Bolen, "1–2 Chronicles," 446.

the certain hope that is to come through David: Since many of his sins and faults would not serve this theme, they are not included.

TEMPLE (2 CHRON 1–9)

After David's death, the stage is set: Due to David's countless preparations, Solomon begins to build the temple immediately after taking the throne. This twenty-year project (2 Chron 8:1) is the focus of 2 Chronicles 1–9 and beyond. Köstenberger and Goswell write: "The account of Solomon's reign is dominated by the building of the temple (2 Chron. 2–8). The better Judean kings reformed the temple (e.g., Joash in 2 Chron. 24:1-14; Hezekiah in 29:3-36). According to the Chronicler, the temple was the locus of worship for both north and south (e.g., 2 Chron. 11:13-17; 15:8-15; 19:4; 30:1-13, 25; 31:1; 34:9)."[13] The temple is clearly a key focal point of the story.

The location of the temple is Mount Moriah, on the threshing floor of Ornan the Jebusite—the very place where the angel of YHWH relented from destroying Jerusalem in response to David's sin (1 Chron 21:15; 2 Chron 3:1). This ornate structure will replace the tabernacle—a building to replace a tent. It will follow a similar pattern as the tabernacle, but with much more grandeur: the finest of materials, including staggering amounts of gold. When the building is complete, the ark of the covenant is finally brought to the temple, with so many sacrificial offerings that they cannot be counted (2 Chron 5). In this place, YHWH's throne will be under the wings of the gold cherubim.

After they put the ark in its place, the priests come out of the holy place, where musicians are playing cymbals, harps, lyres, and 120 trumpets. They also sing in unison the words of the psalmist: "For he is good, for his steadfast love endures forever" (2 Chron 5:13; cf. Ps 100:5, etc.). Next, "the house, the house of the Lord, was filled with

[13]Köstenberger and Goswell, *Biblical Theology*, 331.

a cloud, so that the priests could not stand to minister because of the cloud, for the glory of the LORD filled the house of God" (2 Chron 5:13-14). YHWH has been enthroned above the cherubim in the most holy place.

Next, Solomon blesses the people, emphasizing that with the temple complete, YHWH has fulfilled his promise to David (2 Chron 6:1-11). Then, on his knees and with his hands spread out toward heaven, Solomon prays to dedicate the temple (2 Chron 6:12-42). Most notably, this prayer is infused with Moses' teaching on blessings for covenant keeping, curses for covenant breaking, and restoration for covenant repentance (Lev 26; Deut 28; 30:1-10). For example,

> If they sin against you—for there is no one who does not sin—and you are angry with them and give them to an enemy, so that they are carried away captive to a land far or near, yet if they turn their heart in the land to which they have been carried captive, and repent and plead with you in the land of their captivity, saying, "We have sinned and have acted perversely and wickedly," if they repent with all their heart and with all their soul in the land of their captivity to which they were carried captive, and pray toward their land, which you gave to their fathers, the city that you have chosen and the house that I have built for your name, then hear from heaven your dwelling place their prayer and their pleas, and maintain their cause and forgive your people who have sinned against you. (2 Chron 6:36-39)

For the first readers of Chronicles—those who had returned from exile and were waiting for the full, promised restoration—words like this from the lips of Solomon would have assured them of YHWH's forgiveness and infused them with hope that the beginnings of restoration they had already experienced would be fully realized in the future.

"As soon as Solomon finished his prayer, fire came down from heaven and consumed the burnt offering and the sacrifices, and the glory of the LORD filled the temple. And the priests could not enter the house of the Lord, because the glory of the Lord filled the Lord's house" (2 Chron 7:1-2). The temple is then dedicated, with the sacrifice of 22,000 oxen and 120,000 sheep (2 Chron 7:5). The long-awaited place of permanence for YHWH is now complete.

In the final twenty-seven chapters of Chronicles—the story of the next 345 years of God's people—God's presence will remain the central concern. These chapters tell of periods of decline and reform in temple worship (e.g., Joash in 2 Chron 24:1-14; Hezekiah in 2 Chron 29:3-36), the temple's destruction, and the promise that it will be rebuilt.[14] As we can see, Chronicles is about YHWH dwelling among his people: its beginning, loss, and future restoration. Ultimately, the hope-filled message of Chronicles emphasizes a coming return to Eden, where YHWH will once again dwell among his people.

HOPE (2 CHRON 10–36)

After the death of Solomon, his son Rehoboam takes the throne. His reign quickly leads to the kingdom dividing in two. With Israel in the north and Judah in the south (2 Chron 10:1-19), the author then summarizes, "So Israel has been in rebellion against the house of David to this day" (2 Chron 10:19). In the story that unfolds in the rest of Chronicles, the focus is on Judah and its kings, with appearances by Israel's kings when they help tell the story of Judah.

These last twenty-seven chapters of Chronicles continue the trajectory that began in the story of David (1 Chron 9:35–29:30) and Solomon (2 Chron 1–9): When the sin of Judah's kings serves the story, it is included, but it is sparse. Since Chronicles was written to emphasize hope that the ultimate redemption would be fully accomplished, these chapters are dominated by encouragement.

Just like David's life was not whitewashed by the author of Chronicles (e.g., his sin in taking the census, 1 Chron 21:1), so these

[14]See Köstenberger and Goswell, *Biblical Theology*, 331.

twenty-seven chapters do not gloss over the sins of Judah's kings. For example, we learn that Rehoboam had "eighteen wives and sixty concubines, and fathered twenty-eight sons and sixty daughters" (2 Chron 11:21). More overtly, we learn later that when his rule was established, "he abandoned the law of the LORD, and all Israel with him" (2 Chron 12:1). As a result of this, King Shishak of Egypt enters Judah with his army and "took the fortified cities of Judah and came as far as Jerusalem" (2 Chron 12:4). YHWH then sends Shemaiah the prophet to Rehoboam with a message of judgment: "Thus says the LORD, 'You abandoned me, so I have abandoned you to the hand of Shishak'" (2 Chron 12:5). In response, "the princes of Israel and the king humbled themselves and said, 'The LORD is righteous'" (2 Chron 12:6). What happens next is an exact fulfillment of the earlier prayer of Solomon at the temple dedication (from 1 Chron 6):

> When the LORD saw that they humbled themselves, the word of the LORD came to Shemaiah: "They have humbled themselves. I will not destroy them, but I will grant them some deliverance, and my wrath shall not be poured out on Jerusalem by the hand of Shishak. Nevertheless, they shall be servants to him, that they may know my service and the service of the kingdoms of the countries." (2 Chron 12:7-8)

There are definitely consequences to this sin, even though it is forgiven: Shishak takes away the treasures of YHWH's house and the king's house (2 Chron 12:9). But we are ultimately told that when Rehoboam humbles himself, "the wrath of the LORD turned from him, so as not to make a complete destruction" (2 Chron 12:12).

Most of the kings of Judah are given positive stories, lightly peppered with omissions and sins. For example, Asa is said to have done "what was good and right in the eyes of the LORD his God" (2 Chron 14:2). This includes removing traces of worship to foreign gods and commanding Judah to seek YHWH and to keep his instruction and commands (2 Chron 14:3-4). As a result, we learn that Asa "had no war in those years, for the Lord gave him peace" (2 Chron 14:6). However, we learn later that "the high places were not taken out of Israel," even as "the heart of Asa was wholly true all his days" (2 Chron 15:17). Asa was also prone to rely on human means for deliverance, whether the king of Syria during the threat of war, or physicians (to the neglect of seeking YHWH) during a physical illness (see 2 Chron 16:12).

Among the stories of Judah's kings, Hezekiah and Josiah especially stand out for their monumental reforms. After Ahaz's idolatrous reign, Hezekiah's is marked by his cleansing of the temple, restoring temple worship, the celebration of the Passover, and the restoration of the Levites as leaders in temple worship—all things that were abandoned under the reign of Judah's previous king (and Hezekiah's father), Ahaz. In fact, we are told further that "Hezekiah and all the people rejoiced because God had provided for the people, for the thing came about suddenly" (2 Chron 29:36). Hezekiah also claims his reign over more than just the land of Judah, for "Hezekiah sent to all Israel and Judah, and wrote letters also to Ephraim and Manasseh, that they should come to the house of the Lord at Jerusalem to keep the Passover to the Lord, the God of Israel" (2 Chron 30:1). Once again, the borders of God's people extend to the Northern Kingdom of Israel. Later, the rediscovery of the book of the Torah of YHWH marks the reign of Josiah with humility, repentance, and radical obedience to YHWH (2 Chron 34). Josiah takes away all means of committing idolatry in the land and requires faithfulness to YHWH among all Israel before he also keeps the Passover celebration.

Why did the author of Chronicles take the time to emphasize the Passover celebrations under the leadership of Hezekiah and Josiah? This was to be an annual festival for God's people, to celebrate the final plague before the exodus from Egypt, the night the angel of death passed over the houses of Israelites who had the blood of a lamb splattered on their door frame. By highlighting this festival near the conclusion of his book, the author of Chronicles is signaling hope in a new and better exodus that YHWH will soon accomplish.

This hope is on full display in the final chapter, where we learn that after his people reject warning after warning from his prophets, YHWH brings about their exile from the land:

> Therefore he brought up against them the king of the Chaldeans, who killed their young men with the sword in the house of their sanctuary and had no compassion on young man or virgin, old man or aged. He gave them all into his hand. And all the vessels of the house of God, great and small, and the treasures of the house of the LORD, and the treasures of the king and of his princes, all these he brought to Babylon. And they burned the house of God and broke down the wall of Jerusalem and burned all its palaces with fire and destroyed all its precious vessels. He took into exile in Babylon those who had escaped from the sword, and they became servants to him and to his sons until the establishment of the kingdom of Persia, to fulfill the word of the LORD by the mouth of Jeremiah, until the land had enjoyed its Sabbaths. All the days that it lay desolate it kept Sabbath, to fulfill seventy years. (2 Chron 36:17-21)

However, the book doesn't conclude with disaster. It concludes with God's people on the cusp of restoration:

> Now in the first year of Cyrus king of Persia, that the word of the LORD by the mouth of Jeremiah might be fulfilled, the LORD stirred up the spirit of Cyrus king of Persia, so that he made a proclamation throughout all his kingdom and also put it in writing: "Thus says Cyrus king of Persia, 'The LORD, the God of heaven, has given me all the kingdoms of the earth, and he has charged me to build him a house at Jerusalem, which is in Judah. Whoever is among you of all his people, may the LORD his God be with him. Let him go up.'" (2 Chron 36:22-23)

Once again, hope is the dominant note in 2 Chronicles 10–36 and in fact the entire book. But this hope is not merely local; it is not only for the fledgling nation of Israel who will struggle to rebuild their war-torn temple and land. Köstenberger and Goswell put it well: "When it is noted that Chronicles begins at the point of creation (1 Chron. 1:1) and ends with the prospect of the rebuilding of God's temple and the gathering of all his people in the consummated kingdom of God, it is plain that history will culminate with the open and unchallenged rule of God over all the world."[15] The Old Testament concludes, then, with certain hope in, but not yet the experience of, the ultimate redemption fully accomplished.

LOOKING FORWARD TO CHRIST: THE ULTIMATE REDEMPTION FULLY ACCOMPLISHED

Since Chronicles is a summative book, it is fitting for us to step back and revel together at the way Jesus fulfilled the Old Testament hope.

We have noticed that the Old Testament concludes with certain hope in the ultimate redemption that will be fully accomplished. The New Testament begins the same way the Old Testament ends: with a genealogy. If Chronicles concludes the Old Testament by harking back to Adam and focusing on David, temple, and hope, the New Testament begins with a genealogy that traces the lineage from Abraham to David to the exile to the Messiah, Jesus (Mt 1:1, 17). According to Matthew, the entire Old Testament story of redemption has led to this moment, or better, this *person*. Every Old Testament genealogy has been leading to the birth of the ultimate seed of the woman, Jesus Christ (see Gen 3:15). He will crush the head of the seed of the serpent and win the ultimate victory over sin, death, and hell forever. Since he is born in the lineage of King David, this long-dormant dynasty can be restored with the birth of King Jesus.

In many ways, the experience of God's people leading up to the birth of Jesus was similar to the end of Ezra–Nehemiah: They lived in

---

[15]Köstenberger and Goswell, *Biblical Theology*, 338.

their land, and they had a temple for worship. But they were also missing an essential element: There was no king on David's throne, and they were ruled by a puppet king named Herod, whom the Romans had installed to keep the Jews faithful to Rome. This is why King Herod felt so threatened by a child born as king of the Jews: His rule was in jeopardy by the birth of this child whom the Old Testament had promised would be the ultimate Messiah and Redeemer.

After the exodus and wilderness experiences of Jesus—themes we covered at the end of chapter five—Jesus begins his public ministry. His preaching theme is simple: "Repent, for the kingdom of heaven is at hand" (Mt 4:17). He calls his first followers and ministers to crowds. Not only does Jesus preach the good news of the kingdom, but he also heals "every disease and every affliction among the people" (Mt 4:23). The implication is clear: In his preaching Jesus is announcing the fulfillment of the Old Testament hope, and in his actions he is giving foretastes of a future, ultimate reversal of the effects of the fall into sin (see Gen 3:16-19). Disease and death and demon possession didn't enter human experience until sin entered the world, and with his words and actions Jesus announced that the ultimate redemption was at hand.

After a three-year public ministry, the coronation of King Jesus was near. But instead of accomplishing this with a sword, Jesus does so in his weakness and *death*. The promise in Genesis 3:15 is of mutual deathblows between the seed of the serpent and the seed of the woman. On the cross, the king of the Jews dies (Mt 27:37), and with his last words he quotes the beginning of Psalm 22, "My God, my God, why have you forsaken me?" (Mt 27:46; cf. Ps 22:1). When he dies, the earth shakes and the rocks split (Mt 27:51). All of creation is in the pangs of *rebirth* as the massive, heavy curtain that limited access to God's presence is torn in half *by God* because it is torn *from top to bottom*. Dead bodies of saints are then raised, and a Roman centurion makes the good confession, "Truly this was the Son of God!" (Mt 27:54).

The rest of the story is awe-inspiring. Jesus' body is buried, but death cannot hold him. The sinless Son of God rises from the dead and appears to his followers. He will then ascend to heaven, where he will sit on the throne at God's right hand (see Ps 110:1). But this is gloriously not how the story ends. The death and burial and resurrection and ascension of Jesus usher in the dawn of the new era. As Christians, we now live in light of the victory Jesus has won *for us* over sin, Satan, death, and hell. Spirit-filled and Spirit-empowered believers in Jesus now continue his mission of making disciples as we yearn for the fullness that is guaranteed because it has been purchased by the death of Christ. When Jesus returns and the entire Bible's story is fulfilled, all his people will live in a new heavens and a new earth forever. On that day we will hear an awe-inspiring announcement in a loud voice from the throne, saying, "Behold, the dwelling place of God is with man. He will dwell with them, and they will be his people, and God himself will be with them as their God. He will wipe away every tear from their eyes, and death shall be no more, neither shall there be mourning, nor crying, nor pain anymore, for the former things have passed away" (Rev 21:3-4). Christians live each day with a sense of anticipation, for the one who accomplished these things also said, "Surely I am coming soon" (Rev 22:20).

DISCUSSION QUESTIONS

1. How do Jesus' words in Matthew 23:35 reveal which book should conclude the Old Testament story?
2. Why does Chronicles begin with a genealogy?
3. Which aspects of David's life are emphasized by the author of Chronicles, and how do these differ from David's portrait in Samuel–Kings? How can we explain the different emphases of each work?

4. Share ways that Chronicles emphasizes temple worship. Why is this important?
5. How does 2 Chronicles 10–36 emphasize the theme of hope?
6. Share some ways Jesus fulfilled the Old Testament hope, especially focusing on aspects from the "Looking Forward to Christ" section of this chapter that you had not previously noticed.

CONCLUSION

TAKE UP AND READ!

THE OLD TESTAMENT STORY OF REDEMPTION begins in the Pentateuch and continues through Joshua, Judges, Samuel, Kings, Ruth, Daniel, Esther, Ezra–Nehemiah, and Chronicles.[1] As we learned to unfold the Old Testament story in this order—by following the lead of Jesus and the New Testament authors—we have discovered many fresh insights. We also noticed that the apostle Paul filled *two whole years* of daily teaching about Jesus and the kingdom of God, from Genesis to Chronicles and all the books in between. Every part of the Old Testament bears witness to Christ.

We have learned that a land for God's people is an essential theme from Genesis to Revelation. The book of Joshua realizes this hope in a way that anticipates Jesus as the glorious fulfillment of YHWH dwelling among his people. We now look forward to the new heavens and new earth as the ultimate, earthy, global realization of this promise—one that will be enjoyed for eternity by all who are in Christ.

We learned that the judges came at a time in history when there was no king in Israel, and everyone did what was right in their own eyes (see Judg 17:6; etc.). We witnessed the sin of the community as

[1]While these Old Testament books tell the story of God's people, the books by prophets, poets, and sages that are found in between provide commentary on that story.

the cause of its troubles, and we also watched as God graciously (and repeatedly) raised up judges to deliver his redeemed. Fittingly, we learned to celebrate Jesus as a better deliverer than Samson, one who was (and is) perfectly righteous.

Thankfully, the period of the judges was temporary. We learned that from the beginning, YHWH's plan was to raise up a *king* to lead and represent his redeemed people. Although David's reign was the high point of the Old Testament line of kings, his flawed and temporary rule anticipated King Jesus, who has now taken his seat at the right hand of God on the throne of the cosmos (see Ps 110:1; Lk 20:42-43; etc.). We yearn for the day when every knee will bow, "in heaven and on earth and under the earth, and every tongue confess that Jesus Christ is Lord, to the glory of God the Father" (Phil 2:10-11).

Additionally, we witnessed the emergence of Old Testament prophets, who were given a glimpse into the divine realm and reported these visions to God's people. We learned, though, that in the presence of Jesus, the two greatest Old Testament prophets were told to *listen to him*.

In the division, decline, and exile of God's people, we stood in horror at the downward spiral of covenant breaking and its tragic results. But we did not grieve as those without hope. Armed with Deuteronomy 30:1-10, we anticipated a restoration for covenant repentance. From our new covenant perspective, we know this was fulfilled by the Savior who experienced the ultimate exile (on the cross) for all who would turn from their sins and trust his work for them.

We learned that, in its placement in the earliest attested Hebrew order of Old Testament books, Ruth is a whole lot more (but also not less) than an incredible love story. As the Old Testament story unfolds with Ruth as a preface to the Writings, it leads us to the birth of an anointed king who will be for all peoples, Jew and non-Jew alike. This will find its ultimate fulfillment in the multiethnic chorus of the new heavens and earth (Rev 5:9; 21–22).

The story of sojourn for God's people is told in the books of Daniel and Esther. We focused on the latter and witnessed an out-of-place Jewish man and his younger relative as they navigated the higher ranks of Persia. These sojourning, imperfect Jews were used by YHWH to preserve his exiled people. We also learned that Esther's third-day deliverance from death anticipated the third-day resurrection of Jesus.

Further, we witnessed three waves of return and rebuilding in Ezra–Nehemiah. These were nothing less than the beginnings of restoration for covenant repentance (see Deut 30:1-10). But we also learned to read these books with holy dissatisfaction. This is because Ezra–Nehemiah did not completely fulfill the hope of restoration promised in Deuteronomy 30:1-10, much less the promise of more grandeur the prophets had anticipated (see Ezek 40–48). We also learned that the new covenant teaching of Jesus cut to the heart—more than even the Torah of Moses or the expository preaching of Ezra.

Finally, we witnessed Chronicles as the hope-filled conclusion of the Old Testament story. This book begins with Adam and ends with hope in an ultimate return from exile. Since the restoration in Ezra–Nehemiah left the reader yearning for fullness, Chronicles concludes with the proclamation that the true and ultimate return from exile was cast into the future. We closed that chapter by reveling together in the ultimate restoration that has been accomplished by Christ and that believers will enjoy in its fullness for eternity.

Where do we go from here? This book is not written to provide all the answers to every verse in the Former Prophets and Latter Writings. This book is designed to give a big-picture overview that will help thoughtful Christians like you dig into these books on your own. The goal of this book, then, is to drive us into *the Book* that really matters—God's Word, the Bible. I hope that as we understand the big picture in a deeper way, this will help with a lifetime of profound insights, life-transforming application, and a greater vision of God as we immerse ourselves in his precious Word even more. Take up and read!

ACKNOWLEDGMENTS

This book has its roots in my personal, daily, Bible reading and prayer, in studying the writings of others, and in my classroom ministry at Heritage Theological Seminary. In particular, my understanding of the Old Testament has been especially shaped by the writing ministries of Stephen G. Dempster, Peter J. Gentry, Andreas Köstenberger and Gregory Goswell, Bruce K. Waltke, James M. Hamilton Jr., Jason S. DeRouchie, and Paul R. House. I am also blessed with perceptive students at Heritage Theological Seminary. Their questions and insights have played a significant role in shaping my thinking on this marvelous portion of God's Word.

Thanks also to the following readers of some early chapter drafts who gave feedback and helped to set the trajectory of this work: Adam and Carly Buchwald, Jacob and Roseanne Tomc, Alex Guenther, Kyle Hunter, Emily Vaillancourt, and Natalie Vaillancourt. I am also thankful for feedback on a penultimate draft of the entire book by Daniel Bredin, Bob Kallonen, Jonathan Kroeker, Dennis Anderson, Natalie Vaillancourt, Jonny Atkinson, Sean Sheeran, and Caleb Hall. As my copy and content editor at Heritage Theological Seminary, Carly Buchwald also gave very detailed and helpful feedback. In addition, I am thankful for the guidance of Rachel Hastings, who is my editor at IVP Academic. It is a great pleasure to serve Christ alongside so many amazing people! Their labors greatly improved the theology, clarity, and flow of the book. Every shortcoming that remains is, of course, my own.

It is an absolute delight to serve Christ alongside my wife, Natalie, and with our two awesome kids, Caleb and Emily. What a joy to live in a house where four people are seeking to honor and serve the Lord! For this reason, each of them has shaped the author of this book in more ways than they could ever imagine.

Finally, I praise God that he broke into my life and shone into my heart "the light of the gospel of the glory of Christ, who is the image of God" (2 Cor 4:4). This book is written by a saved sinner who is passionate about making much of him!

BIBLIOGRAPHY

Alter, Robert. *The Hebrew Bible: A Translation with Commentary*. 3 vols. Norton, 2019.

Beckwith, Roger. *The Old Testament Canon of the New Testament Church and Its Background in Early Judaism*. Eerdmans, 1986.

Beldman, David J. H. *Deserting the King: The Book of Judges*. Transformative Word. Lexham, 2017.

Block, Daniel I. *Ruth: A Discourse Analysis of the Hebrew Bible*. Zondervan Exegetical Commentary on the Old Testament. Zondervan Academic, 2015.

Blomberg, Craig, Thomas Schreiner, and Miles Van Pelt. *A Guide to Biblical Theology*. N.d. www.biblicaltraining.org/learn/academy/bt201-a-guide-to-biblical-theology.

Bolen, Todd. "1–2 Chronicles." In *What the Old Testament Authors Really Cared About: A Survey of Jesus' Bible*, edited by Jason S. DeRouchie, 442-62. Kregel Academic, 2013.

Bronner, Leila Leah. *The Stories of Elijah and Elisha as Polemics Against Baal Worship*. Brill, 1968.

Carson, D. A. "Matthew." Pages 23-670 in *Matthew, Mark, Luke*. Edited by Tremper Longman III and David E. Garland. The Expositor's Bible Commentary 9. Zondervan Academic, 1984.

Dempster, Stephen G. *Dominion and Dynasty: A Theology of the Hebrew Bible*. New Studies in Biblical Theology 15. InterVarsity Press, 2003.

Dempster, Stephen G. "From Slight Peg to Cornerstone to Capstone: The Resurrection of Christ on 'The Third Day' According to the Scriptures." *Westminster Theological Journal* 76, no. 2 (2014): 371-409.

Dempster, Stephen G. *The Return of the Kingdom: A Biblical Theology of God's Reign*. IVP Academic, 2024.

Dempster, Stephen G. "A Wandering Moabite: Ruth—A Book in Search of a Canonical Home." In *The Shape of the Writings*, edited by Julius Steinberg and Timothy J. Stone, 87-118. Siphrut 16. Eisenbrauns, 2015.

DeRouchie, Jason S. "The Hermeneutical Significance of the Shape of the Christian Canon." In *The Law, the Prophets, and the Writings: Studies in Evangelical Old*

Testament Hermeneutics in Honor of Duane A. Garrett, edited by Andrew M. King, William R. Osborne, and Joshua M. Philpot, 29-56. B&H Academic, 2021.

DeRouchie, Jason S., and Daryl Aaron. "Ezra–Nehemiah." In *What the Old Testament Authors Really Cared About: A Survey of Jesus' Bible*, edited by Jason S. DeRouchie, 428-41. Kregel Academic, 2013.

Duke, Alex, James M. Hamilton Jr., and Sam Emadi. "On Opening Up Your Mind to Something You've Never Considered—Or, the Weirdest Episode of Bible Talk Yet." *Bible Talk* (podcast), May 3, 2023. www.9marks.org/conversations/on-opening-up-your-mind-to-something-youve-never-considered-or-the-weirdest-episode-of-bible-talk-yet-bible-talk-ep-82/.

Enns, Peter E. *Exodus*. New International Version Application Commentary. Zondervan Academic, 2000.

Firth, David G. *The Message of Esther*. Bible Speaks Today. IVP Academic, 2010.

Firth, David G., and Brittany N. Melton, eds. *Reading Esther Intertextually*. The Library of Hebrew Bible/Old Testament Studies 725. T&T Clark, 2022.

Fowler, Donald, and Jason S. DeRouchie. "1–2 Kings." In *What the Old Testament Authors Really Cared About: A Survey of Jesus' Bible*, edited by Jason S. DeRouchie, 218-37. Kregel Academic, 2013.

Gallagher, Edmon L., and John D. Meade. *The Biblical Canon Lists from Early Christianity: Texts and Analysis*. Oxford University Press, 2017.

Gentry, Peter J., and Stephen J. Wellum. *Kingdom Through Covenant: A Biblical-Theological Understanding of the Covenants*. 2nd ed. Crossway, 2018.

Grenz, Stanley J., David Guretzki, and Cherith Fee Nordling. *Pocket Dictionary of Theological Terms*. IVP Academic, 1999.

Grisham, John. *Camino Island*. Vintage, 2018.

Hallo, William W., ed. *The Context of Scripture*. Brill, 1997–2002.

Hamilton, James M., Jr. *God's Glory in Salvation Through Judgment: A Biblical Theology*. Crossway, 2010.

Hamilton, James M., Jr. "The Skull Crushing Seed of the Woman: Inner-Biblical Interpretation of Genesis 3:15." *The Southern Baptist Journal of Theology* 10, no. 2 (2006): 30-54.

Hamilton, Victor P. *The Book of Genesis: Chapters 1–17*. New International Commentary on the Old Testament. Eerdmans, 1990.

Harris, W. Hall, ed. *The NET Bible Notes*. Biblical Studies Press, 2005.

Hill, Andrew E. *1 & 2 Chronicles*. New International Version Application Commentary. Zondervan, 2003.

Hill, Andrew E., and John H. Walton. *A Survey of the Old Testament*. 4th ed. Zondervan Academic, 2023.

"Hoover Dam." Water Education Foundation, n.d. www.watereducation.org/aquapedia/hoover-dam.

House, Paul R. *Old Testament Theology*. InterVarsity Press, 1998.

Isaacson, Walter. *Steve Jobs*. Simon & Schuster, 2021.

Janzen, Waldemar. "Geography of Faith: A Christian Perspective on the Meaning of Places." *Studies in Religion* 3, no. 2 (1973): 166-82.

Jobes, Karen H. *Esther*. New International Version Application Commentary. Zondervan Academic, 1999.

Kaiser, Walter C., Jr. *The Christian and the Old Testament*. William Carey Library, 2012.

Kidner, Derek. *Ezra and Nehemiah*. Tyndale Old Testament Commentary. InterVarsity Press, 2009.

King, Philip J., and Lawrence E. Stager. *Life in Biblical Israel*. Westminster John Knox, 2001.

Kinkade, Thomas. *Thomas Kinkade Special Collector's Edition 2024 Deluxe Wall Calendar with Print: Lakeside Splendor*. Andrews McMeel, 2023.

Köstenberger, Andreas J., and Gregory Goswell. *Biblical Theology: A Canonical, Thematic, and Ethical Approach*. Crossway, 2023.

Leggett, Donald A. *Loving God and Disturbing Men: Preaching from the Prophets*. Baker, 1990.

Levering, Matthew. *Ezra & Nehemiah*. Brazos Theological Commentary on the Bible. Brazos, 2023.

Martin, Oren. *Bound for the Promised Land*. New Studies in Biblical Theology 34. IVP Academic, 2015.

Miller, Chris A., and Jason S. DeRouchie. "Ruth." In *What the Old Testament Authors Really Cared About: A Survey of Jesus' Bible*, edited by Jason S. DeRouchie, 326-35. Kregel Academic, 2013.

Moore, George Foot. *A Critical and Exegetical Commentary on Judges*. International Critical Commentary. Scribner's, 1895.

Payne, J. Barton. *The Theology of the Older Testament*. Zondervan, 1962.

Phillips, E. A. "Esther 6: Person." In *Dictionary of the Old Testament: Wisdom, Poetry and Writings*, edited by Tremper Longman III and Peter Enns, 188-93. InterVarsity Press, 2008.

Pritchard, James B., ed. *Ancient Near Eastern Texts Relating to the Old Testament*. 3rd ed. Princeton University Press, 1969.

Richter, Sandra L. *The Epic of Eden: A Christian Entry into the Old Testament*. IVP Academic, 2008.

Rosner, Brian S. "Idolatry." In *New Dictionary of Biblical Theology*, edited by T. Desmond Alexander and Brian S. Rosner, 569-75. InterVarsity Press, 2000.

Schnittjer, Gary Edward, and Matthew S. Harmon. *How to Study the Bible's Use of the Bible: Seven Hermeneutical Choices for the Old and New Testaments*. Zondervan Academic, 2024.

Seevers, Boyd. "Joshua." In *What the Old Testament Authors Really Cared About: A Survey of Jesus' Bible*, edited by Jason S. DeRouchie, 172-85. Kregel Academic, 2013.

Shogren, Gary S. "Redemption: New Testament." In *Anchor Bible Dictionary*, edited by David Noel Freedman, 5:654-57. Doubleday, 1992.

Smith, Gary V. "Esther." In *What the Old Testament Authors Really Cared About: A Survey of Jesus' Bible*, edited by Jason S. DeRouchie, 420-27. Kregel Academic, 2013.

Taylor, Marion Ann. *Ruth, Esther*. Story of God Bible Commentary. Zondervan Academic, 2020.

Vaillancourt, Ian J. *David, Goliath, and the Gospel: Living in Light of Our Savior's Victory*. Discovery Series. Our Daily Bread Ministries, 2021.

Vaillancourt, Ian J. *The Dawning of Redemption: The Story of the Pentateuch and the Hope of the Gospel*. Crossway, 2022.

Vaillancourt, Ian J. *Treasuring the Psalms: How to Read the Songs That Shape the Soul of the Church*. IVP Academic, 2023.

Waltke, Bruce K., and Charles Yu. *An Old Testament Theology: An Exegetical, Canonical, and Thematic Approach*. Zondervan, 2007.

Webb, Barry G. *Five Festal Garments: Christian Reflections on the Song of Songs, Ruth, Lamentations, Ecclesiastes, and Esther*. New Studies in Biblical Theology 10. InterVarsity Press, 2000.

Wenham, Gordon J. *Genesis 1–15*. Word Biblical Commentary. Zondervan, 1987.

SCRIPTURE INDEX

ALSO BY IAN J. VAILLANCOURT

Treasuring the Psalms
978-1-5140-0510-1